Goodbye Stalin

A True Story of Wars, Escapes and Reinventions

Sigrid von Bremen Thomas

Durban House Press

Printed in the United States of America.

For information address:
Durban House Publishing Company, Inc.
7502 Greenville Avenue, Suite 500
Dallas, Texas 75231

Library of Congress Cataloging-in-Publication Data

Thomas, Sigrid von Bremen, 1931 -

Goodbye Stalin / Sigrid von Bremen Thomas

1. von Bremen Thomas, Sigrid, 1931—Childhood and Youth
2. World War, 1939-1945—Personal Narratives, Estonian
3. World War, 1939-1945—Personal Narratives, Baltic German
4. Refugees, World War, 1939-1945—Estonian—Baltic German
5. History, European, 20th Century—Baltic German
6. Displaced Persons, 1948-1956—United States—Immigration
7. Children—Baltic German—Estonian—Biography
I. Title

Library of Congress Control Number: 2007929252

ISBN: 0-9779863-4-9

First Edition

Visit our Web site at http://www.durbanhouse.com

To my children, Karina and Stryk

1939 and Present-Day Boundaries of Eastern Europe

Trek Route from Poland to Germany

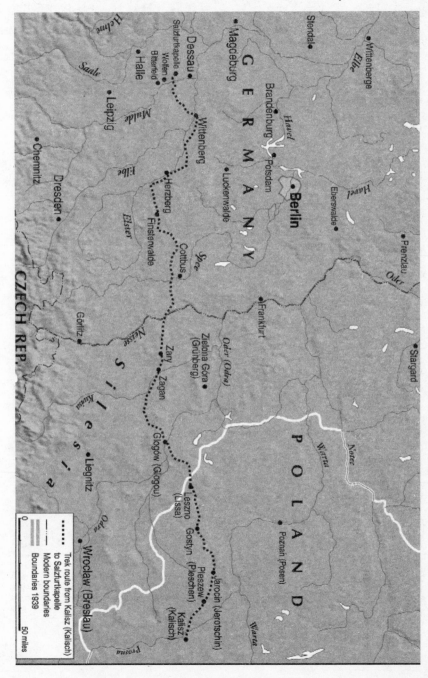

Acknowledgements

I owe thanks to many people for help in the writing of this memoir. It is too late to thank my parents, and in particular my father, for keeping journals and diaries throughout his life. Without these written words I would have never been able to write this book. I'm grateful to my brother Ulf for filling in some of the details of our childhood, which I had long forgotten or never knew. I much appreciate the conversations and support I received from my cousin Karin and her husband Dave.

In particular I thank my long-time friend, Irmgard Hunt, author of *On Hitler's Mountain–Overcoming the Legacy of a Nazi Childhood*, and Frank Joseph, author of *To Love Mercy*. They provided expert guidance through the complicated world of publishing. Several workshops at the Writer's Center in Bethesda, Maryland, and the Washington Independent Writers in Washington, D.C., were crucial for developing my writing skills, and the outline of the book.

I will be forever grateful to my manuscript editor, Robert Middlemiss, who believed in this book from the moment it reached his eyes.

My deepest thanks go to my husband and initial reader, who never wavered in his belief that I could write *Goodbye Stalin*. I thank him for not being heavy-penciled but a sensitive editor in helping with first revisions. His love and patience sustained me in moments of doubt and frustration.

My final note of gratitude goes to the Refugee Relief Act of 1953 and to Alice Kandarian, my American sponsor. Thank you, America.

Introduction

This memoir celebrates a family whose fortunes were blown up by history—not once or twice, but four times. I have written it because everyone to whom I told a few of my stories urged that I put the whole tale on paper. "Your family survived real life *Gone with the Winds*," as a friend once said. Even Margaret Mitchell, creator of Scarlett O'Hara, might have been amazed.

The framework of the book is my personal coming of age story, from childhood in the 1930s to young womanhood in the 1950s. Wrapped inside are flashbacks to my parents' and grandmother's earlier and equally tumultuous lives. Our family went from feudal glory under the czars through revolution in 1917, then democracy in Estonia, Nazism in Poland during World War II, communism in East Germany, and finally freedom in West Germany and the United States. We compressed 250 years of European political and social history into a third of a century. Readers of my story witness the greatest events of modern Europe up close through our own eyes. No textbook can match this intimacy and vividness.

My story also recaptures two vast human migrations now lost to history. At the end of World War II, some 13 million Eastern Europeans fled or were expelled from eastern Germany, Poland, Czechoslovakia and a dozen other countries. Most of these were Germans or ethnic Germans. But hundreds of thousands of other nationalities, including Jews, were borne along. They came from Estonia and Latvia in the north to Romania, Moldavia and Bulgaria in the south. Their sufferings, deaths and dislocation are still dwarfed by the unique horrors of the Holocaust. But the exodus did represent the largest mass migration of human beings in 1500 years.

Once in Germany, many of these refugees were unable or unwilling to make a final home. So 600,000 of us, over and above the ordinary immigration quotas, were permitted to come to the United

States by two special acts of Congress. I am proud and grateful to have been among this number. Jews, Poles, Czechs, Hungarians, Slovaks, Russians—whatever—we made up the last mass migration of Europeans to America. Almost no one in the United States today knows about us. Now they will.

Sigrid von Bremen Thomas
Potomac, Maryland

Foreword

I have known Sigrid von Bremen Thomas for nearly a quarter of a century, but in all those years, I knew her only as Sigrid Thomas —and the "von Bremen" contains a story of war and survival that I would have scarcely guessed. Her engaging and frightening memoir transports us back to a world that seems far removed from our own and yet is disturbingly relevant. By all rights, Sigrid von Bremen Thomas should not have survived to tell this tale, retrieved from the depths of her consciousness, old scrapbooks and faded letters. Indeed, she might never have been born; before her birth, the new revolutionary government in Russia arrested her father and imprisoned him in Siberia, where he might have died. During World War II, she and her mother were strafed by fighters as they fled Poland. More than once, they could have died of starvation. Later she escaped under gunfire from East to West Germany. Only after that did she immigrate to the United States, become a photography editor for *Life* magazine, marry and raise two children in suburban Maryland.

The connection between this world and our own lies in the huge potential for human suffering inflicted on vast masses of ordinary people by political and ideological fanatics. In Sigrid's childhood and adolescence, the fanatics embraced fascism, Nazism and communism. In the present era, they preach radical Islam. But the result was (and is) the same: disorder, chaos, destruction and death. This is not a political memoir. Sigrid's parents simply wished to be left alone to live their lives. Here is the parallel with our own era, when people strive to preserve the familiar, personal and intimate in the face of frightful dangers. The main difference between then and now is the scale of tragedy.

Sigrid von Bremen was born in Tallinn, Estonia in 1931. Even now, it's doubtful that many Americans can locate Estonia on a

map. It's little more than a speck of a country, present population
1.3 million, which stretches along the eastern coast of the Baltic
Sea, just across the Strait of Finland from Helsinki and not far
west from St. Petersburg in Russia. Her parents were descended
from German Teutonic knights who, having first invaded in the
13th century, became the country's landed aristocracy. The von
Bremens' estate, Avanduse, was 21 square miles and included three
villages. As members of the privileged class, Sigrid's parents in-
stinctively disdained politics; any change was—for them—likely to
be for the worse.

So it was. Estonia became independent after World War I (it
had belonged to czarist Russia), and its new democratic government—a coalition of center left and center right parties—expro-
priated Avanduse along with most other estates owned by their
German overlords. Only a legal loophole enabled the family to re-
tain a much smaller 120-acre estate, Solitude, that had been used as
a summer retreat. Still, her parents adapted; they created a thriving
business of raising vegetables and flowers in greenhouses.

Then came the notorious German-Soviet Union Non-
Aggression Pact of August 23, 1939: Hitler's green light to invade
Poland. The pact carved up Eastern Europe between Germany and
the Soviet Union, which received the Baltic states (Estonia, Latvia
and Lithuania). For the von Bremens, this could have been a death
sentence. As members of the former czarist aristocracy, they
would be enemies of the state and shipped off to labor camps or
worse.

We Americans often see war as a collision between good and
evil—and certainly World War II was that. But even in this most
righteous of conflicts, moral ambiguities abounded. Sigrid's parents were not Nazis and, by all evidence, detested Hitler; but their
survival and well-being depended on the Nazis. As part of the secret
German-Soviet diplomacy, Stalin had agreed to allow Hitler to
evacuate the German communities in the Baltic states. The refugees
were to be resettled in now-occupied Poland as part of Hitler's

plan to Germanize as much of Europe as possible. On Nov. 4, Thomas, her mother, grandmother and brother sailed for Poland; her father joined them later. The moral ambiguities quickly multiplied. They were called *Rückwanderer* ("returnees"). "Returnees to where?" her mother asked. "It's been centuries since we left Germany." In school, students were instructed "to greet each teacher by raising our rights arms only a little above the level of our shoulder and simultaneously shouting '*Heil Hitler*.'"

In the spring of 1940, the von Bremens received a 540-acre estate seized from a Polish family. Thomas's mother felt guilty. With difficulty, she located the previous owners, who had moved to an apartment in Warsaw, and shipped them their silver and some personal possessions. Sigrid confesses that her early years in Poland, riding around on the farm's horses and playing with her friends, were "among the happiest of my life." But she also befriended the farm's Polish blacksmith, who brandishes a small statue. "My hero, Jozef Pilsudski. A great revolutionary," he said one day. "It's because of him that we were freed from the czar. I wish he were still alive—to free us one more time." Sobering stuff, even for a nine-year-old. After that, Sigrid visited the blacksmith less often.

It is in these small details of everyday life that we glimpse the realities of war that are often omitted in the sweeping histories of grand strategy and massive battles. What we forget is that, for most people, war merely complicates and overlays everything else in their lives. Tolstoy said that all happy families are alike and that every unhappy family is unhappy in its own way, but the truth is that—happy, unhappy or both—every family is hostage to itself. Sigrid's memoir is compelling precisely because it seamlessly weaves together the pleasures and sorrows of her family—her domineering grandmother, her rebellious brother, her reserved mother and commanding father—with the war's losses.

There is more than a little drama here. At war's end, Sigrid and her brother Ulf accidentally stumble upon the diary of a young woman who has come to work for the family—and discover that she has fallen in love with their father and that the two are having an affair. The discovery "left a considerably bigger impact on me than either Hitler's suicide or the end of the war," she writes. Some weeks later, Sigrid and Ulf managed to get their mother alone:

> We told her. She sat in silence, wiping her eyes. Neither then nor later did she ever acknowledge or deny the relationship that existed between my father and Fräulein von Voigt. Mother finally got up, took a deep breath, and walked out …Nothing changed in our family, we just continued as before.

Never underestimate the human capacity for denial. Just as Sigrid's mother preferred the security of a compromised relationship to the possibility of none at all, her father doggedly defended the family's aristocratic heritage—against all logic and evidence. When advancing Soviet troops forced flight from Poland, the family left in four wagons and a coach stacked high with the family's silverware, paintings and clothing. Much of what they took was soon abandoned. The von Bremens were caught in a panicky, chaotic trek of millions of people westward, intermingled with retreating German soldiers who were attacked relentlessly by the Soviets. The family was lucky to survive. But the self-evident futility of the effort to save its treasures testifies powerfully to the poignant urges of the human heart.

It also expresses the triumph of hope over intelligence, because Sigrid's father—Karl Ernst William—is a shrewd man and keen observer. He had never met Americans, but when advancing U.S. troops arrived in a village where the family had fled, he took their measure. "They are tall athletic figures with free swinging gaits —no rigid military bearing—the greatest possible contrast to the German military," he wrote in his diary. He marveled at their logistical support, the plentiful supply of canned goods particularly. "They take comfortable material existence for granted… Whether the dazzling material situation of the American soldiers brings them to a higher spiritual level, however—that I doubt... one man is so completely like the other in equality of morals, habits of life and so on that it creates a flatness of spirit and intellect." These insights echo de Tocqueville.

It is a wonderful, gripping and painful story. I read it on many levels: as a family saga; as a young girl's voyage to maturity; as an essay in the innocent suffering of war; as a history of the little-known (among Americans) German collapse in Eastern Europe; and as a warning of how easily the props of civilization can fall away. It was rewarding on every one.

Robert J. Samuelson

Robert J. Samuelson's columns for *Newsweek* and *The Washington Post* are syndicated to about 50 U.S. and 20 foreign papers. He is the author of *The Good Life and Its Discontents: the American Dream in the Age of Entitlement, 1945-1995*, and *Untruth: Why the Conventional Wisdom Is (Almost Always) Wrong*.

Chapter 1

On a brilliantly brisk day in early September of 1990, a Soviet KGB officer took me and my husband on a walk along the beach of Türisalu near Keila Joa in northern Estonia. The Soviet officer was determined to prove that the house in which I had grown up had never existed.

"I know every inch of this rotten coastline and I know that there has never been a house in this area," said Major Petrov.

I showed him again my black and white photo. It pictured our simple, shingle-roofed, two-century-old house, built in fieldstone and wood, nestled in an opening in the woods above a panoramic expanse of beach with the lighthouse of Paldiski in the distance. All three of us were now walking on that same sandy beach.

There was one difference. The beach was now a restricted frontier patrolled by a KGB border unit. It was off-limits to any civilian traffic, and Major Petrov was bending the rules. I told him that when my parents moved into the old farmhouse it had been badly infested with bugs. It took my parents weeks to sulfur the pests out of the rooms. But the major was not amused.

Instead he badgered me again: "So you think it is here, or maybe over there?" The major waved one arm, then the other. "What's the matter with you," he asked, "can't you even find your own birthplace? I told you that there is nothing here. All I can say is, you're *kaput*." He twirled a finger around his ear.

I almost doubted myself for a second. Yet I surely had spent my childhood on this stretch of coastline. I had been forced to leave by events leading up to World War II.

Nazi Germany and the Soviet Union had signed a non-aggression pact dividing Eastern Europe into German and Soviet spheres of influence in August of 1939. The Soviet Union got Estonia, gaining the right to occupy the country. My parents would face arrest. They were nobility, a ruling class of ancient German origin that had arrived as Teutonic knights seven centuries earlier. They had survived the fall of the czar and had rebuilt their fortunes as greenhouse growers in newly independent Estonia. But they were unlikely to survive Stalin. So we were among those who had to pack up practically overnight and move to Nazi-occupied Poland in the fall of 1939. World War II, the Cold War and a Soviet ban on all foreign travel outside the capital of Estonia had prevented me from looking for my birthplace until now.

The beach we walked on looked and smelled just as I remembered it. Nothing had changed. Untouched fir woods and stones and sand. The rich aroma of seaweed fermenting in saltwater and sun was still everywhere. Solitude's 120 acres stretched for an entire mile along the water. But had I really come to the right place? The Soviet officer's badgering did not help. He was dead sure that there

Solitude in the 1920s.

had never been a house here. I tried not to listen to his nagging.

Suddenly I stopped in my tracks. The configuration of the shore and woods seemed just right. I looked up at the steep ridge that closed off the horizon to the southeast. "My house must be there, halfway up the bank." Goosebumps covered my arms. "Let's go and look for it under the trees." I pointed with my finger.

"All right, if you insist." The major was still quarrelsome. "We'll climb up there and we'll find nothing."

We found nothing. No remnants of a foundation, no sign of human habitation. Could fifty years wipe out everything?

Well, there was something. An old apple tree. But honestly, I couldn't remember ever seeing one in our garden before. I would surely have remembered if there had been one. I was shaken by the lack of memory. I was so confused that I thought I was losing my mind. Major Petrov certainly thought I was.

"I told you so, didn't I?" he triumphed. "I never make mistakes. I didn't make one when I fought in Afghanistan and I didn't make one here. It's only the *apparatchiks* who make mistakes. Like with their promise to give me a television set. I was supposed to be awarded one for being a hero in Afghanistan. I risked my life. I was wounded. I can show you," he said.

"No, no," I heard myself say. "I don't want to see any scars."

"I'm a nobody now," he continued, "stationed here in this God-forsaken place, and I still have no TV."

Why was he telling me all this? I had my own problems right now. Even Richard, my husband, had begun to nag.

"Gee, think, Sigrid, you've got to remember something of this," he said. He threw a hand at the woods running down to the beach.

"Oh, please! Don't you think I'm trying? It's been fifty years!"

I'd better get hold of myself, I thought, or I'm going to cry. Getting this escorted hike from Major Petrov already seemed a miracle. Travel by westerners outside of Tallinn was at this point only six months old. We had flown in via Aeroflot from Leningrad and picked up one of only five rent-a-cars in the whole country. No road maps were available. None. Estonia, considered a frontier military zone, still crawled with Soviet soldiers, sailors and KGB border troops like Petrov's. Maps were military secrets. Forewarned, we had obtained an Estonian Road Atlas, printed in 1938. All roads had long since been renumbered. We got around by following occasional direction signs to the next town, and by counting the number of intersections we would have to pass before reaching our next turnoff. Our 1938 atlas even showed the sites of every gas station in the country. Some of the marked stations were no longer there, but not one new one had opened in more than fifty years.

Driving from Tallinn to Keila Joa, we were confused by a new, unmapped road. It bore off to the left, detouring us for a few miles before reaching Keila Joa. In town, we asked about Solitude, but drew blank stares. We prowled about the village in low gear, finally finding a small road that seemed headed to the beach, the right direction. But it never looked familiar, and coming around a blind curve, we were stopped by an imposing chain link gate and a sentry house. The gate was topped by barbed wire and emblazoned with two red Soviet stars, beyond which we could see a military base.

A soldier with the red epaulets of KGB border troops and a Kalishnikov slung over his dirty uniform stepped out of the guard house. I explained my mission and showed him old photographs of my house. He just shook his head and said, "You can't come in here. It is restricted."

I pleaded with him. Eventually, the guard became so exasperated that he went back to his sentry box and called from a phone. Minutes passed. The Soviets still controlled Estonia, and in this place we could be—probably were—trespassing. My East German dread of the KGB welled up. Spies? Were we going to be arrested?

Richard, oblivious to my fear, climbed up an embankment to look further into the camp. He must be mad, I thought. Unless he was trying to get both of us killed on the spot. The guard yelled at him to come down.

Finally, after what seemed like an eternity, an officer in a rumpled uniform walked up from the barracks. He was not armed.

"I'm trying to find the house in which I was born. I'm sure it's along the beach here, a little to the north." I showed him my photographs.

"There is no house here," the officer said.

"But there has to be," I exclaimed. "Look at the pictures. In them you see the Paldiski lighthouse, just as you see it over there to the left."

"No house!" He was getting impatient.

"Maybe all that is left is a crumbling foundation," I insisted.

Hostility darkened his face. "*Nyet,*" he said, and started to walk away. But then his eyes settled on the shiny new Volvo.

"All right, we'll drive in your car."

As we got into the car, he introduced himself as Major Mikhail Petrov. With him came the smell of sweat turned stale from his uniform's armpits. The effect was overwhelming. I pressed the electronic button to open a window.

"Wow!" he said.

We drove in silence through the intimidating gate and passed an outdoor physical training area. The parallel bars, half hidden by waist-high weeds, had almost rusted away. Further along, a heavy machine gun, shockingly, squatted on a tripod inside a rotting sand bag emplacement, its muzzle pointed out over the water in the vague direction of Finland, forty miles away. Was this all that was left of the once victorious Soviet Army?

Passing the barracks, we were cheered by men who had rushed to the windows. The soldiers looked as if they had just gotten out of bed, some still in their underwear. They seemed to think it both hilarious and hard to believe that their commander was driving through their base with two Cold War enemies in a Swedish car. The commander ignored them and grimly motioned us to continue ahead on the narrow road through the woods. Suddenly our car came to an abrupt stop. A tree had fallen across the path.

"Now we'll have to walk to the beach and look for your house, which I know does not exist," the major said.

We had still not found the limestone cliffs that I clearly remembered sheltering our house. But the major abruptly halted. "Enough, no more, now we go back," he declared, reversing his stride. I protested, but he remained firm. On our silent walk back to the car, the major's mood suddenly changed. He sidled up to me, smiling mischievously. He must have thought of a new form of torture.

"I'm sorry that I couldn't help you find your house," he said. "But I would like to make a deal with you for letting you come into this restricted area. Maybe you could buy me a television in the hard currency store in Tallinn." When I looked uncomprehending, he added, "You know, TVs are not available to suckers like me. Only you, an *Amerikanski,* can shop at the dollar store. They have plenty of them there."

He said that he would pay me back in rubles, even at the black market rate.

"I will have to think about that," I said.

Why should I make him a favor? All those rubles would be useless to me. The most compelling reason to turn him down was my feeling toward the KGB. After all, I had been trapped under them in East Germany for six years as a teenager following World War II. Communist secret police had also once been responsible for the arrest and deportation of my father. I will not forget his stories of hunger, brutality and relentless winter during a long trip in cattle cars to Siberia in October of 1917.

But it was so wonderful to be back on this beach that I did not want to linger in bad memories. My thoughts drifted to happier times. My family's supposedly idyllic summers here became the subject of a German best seller, *Die Kinder am Meer* (Children by the Sea). It was written by a distant uncle, Carl von Bremen, who spent a season with us in the early 1930s. He fell in love with Solitude, which in his book he called Tizo. He dedicated *Die Kinder am Meer* to me—Dolly. That is how he called me in the book. Later,

Solitude, as illustrated in *Die Kinder am Meer* (*Children by the Sea*).

when I had learned to read, I loved to find out about my fictional self, and secretly wished my name to be Dolly. I was too young to make real-world distinctions. I believed the fiction to be fact. I had no idea as a child that for Grandmama, Mother, and my only brother, life had hardly been as idyllic as described.

My brother Ulf, a sensitive child, was ignored by my father, beaten by his tutor for failing lessons, then sent off at the age of eight to a private boarding school run by a Protestant minister. For my mother, life with her mother-in-law was often an ordeal, causing her migraine headaches and bouts of depression. From the start, Grandmama thought my mother unworthy of her son and found her incompetent ever after. All the adults knew this; I only figured it out later. My mother was lovely when well. Once when we were together, splurging on cakes at Café Stude in Tallinn, I remember the way she looked at me and licked, and licked again, her ice cream spoon. It may have been the first time I had a glimpse of her in a rare moment of innocent mischief.

Grandmama had been looking for simplicity and serenity when she bought the property as a summer residence in 1899. She had a strong need to avoid the conventional. She loved Solitude, as she named it, for its landscape, but she loved even more that it was not a fashionable resort. After her two months of Solitude, she gladly returned to the grand life at Avanduse, the family seat, and to her exotic escapes in Italy. And when that all came crashing down, Solitude itself was saved by a quirk in the law.

How I had feared Grandmama when my brother and I had to go to her house. (*Children by the Sea,* of course, had never mentioned this difficult Grandmama.) She lived in a charming wooden house a short walking distance through the woods from our farmhouse. On Sunday afternoons, Grandmama served hot chocolate to her only two grandchildren. It was always a command performance for which we had to dress in identical button-on sailor suits. We were told not to touch anything but to sit up straight, and not spill. We drank from tiny, precious Meissen cups, with no offer for seconds.

"It's not like it used to be," Grandmama always sighed as we sipped our chocolate.

Major Petrov, my husband and I were forced to re-cross the shallows of a creek, gurgling down through the woods and onto the beach. Wait! This must be the little creek that had gushed passed Grandmama's house. If the creek was still here, her house must be a short way upstream.

I asked the major if I could go and look for it.

"*Nyet*! You've had all the looking you will get," he answered. "Everything here is off-limits."

His face lit up again. "I hope that you have not forgotten the television set I talked about. Maybe I can make a special arrangement and let you look for your grandmother's *dacha*. As I said before, the area is restricted."

I answered that I could not promise anything, but that I would call him the next morning.

"Then the search is over," he said.

I was in agony. My husband, stalling for time, picked up a flat stone from the beach and turned toward the sea. He skimmed it along the quiet water. *Die Kinder am Meer* said that this was one of my skills. A novelist's lie. I learned how to skip stones only when I was much older than Dolly in the book.

But where, I mused, were at least the foundations of Solitude? And of my father's many greenhouses?

We climbed back into the Volvo. The major was still pleading for his TV when we dropped him off at the gate.

I checked the dollar store in the lobby of our hotel, the Viru, when we returned to Tallinn. There was a $400 price tag on the cheapest television set. This meant that he would have to pay us 6,500 rubles, rubles that were mostly useless to us because our trip, booked through the Soviet travel agency Intourist, demanded dollars. The next day, I called him at the arranged time. He picked up the phone before the first ring ended, then hung up on me when I gave him the bad news.

That was my last encounter with the 20th century dictatorships that had uprooted my family three times and ruled my young life. The Soviets and their KGB withdrew from Estonia in 1994, and my husband and I came back the following spring. Supplied with a decent modern map, we approached Solitude from a different direction and easily found the overgrown remnants of the house. We would have found it in 1990 if Major Petrov had allowed us to walk another 200 yards. The sweeping view over a sparkling sea was still there, from the lighthouse in the southwest at Paldiski, a pencil line standing in the horizon, to the shoulder of the limestone cliffs nearby to the northeast. The wildflowers of my childhood were still there. The crumbling foundations of our house and greenhouses blazed with throngs of white anemones mixed with yellow cowslips and lavender-blue hepatica. Saplings of paper birch showed their first chartreuse foliage. Hundreds of migrating white swans honked among the rocks on the beach. Nature was putting on the spectacular show that it had always staged for us after the long northern winter of darkness and gray. A feeling of peace and closure came over me. I cried with happiness. Surrounded by the energies of a bursting spring, my husband and I celebrated with a picnic lunch while we sat on the ancient stones that had formed the walls of my childhood home.

Chapter 2

My father was on a business trip in East Prussia when Hitler invaded Poland on September 1, 1939. He rushed home. I remember his worried face when he tried to get some news from his battery-powered radio. The few news stations he could get were often interrupted by static, leaving him frustrated and angry. Anxiety clouded my mother's face as she leaned close over his shoulder. As my father later recalled, "There was nothing but uncertainty. The tumult of news reports, rumors, and government pronouncements in those first weeks was indescribable."

I recall one phone conversation from these early days vividly. After a shouted exchange on the telephone, my father turned to my mother:

"That was Herr Ivanovich. He cancelled his Christmas orders for cyclamens. He said that we're going to have a war and nobody will be interested in buying flowers."

Herr Ivanovich was my parents' wholesaler in Tallinn.

I had only a dim awareness of the great events then unfolding. But to my parents, they came like blows from a hammer. On September 17, Russia joined Hitler in the attack on Poland, seizing the eastern third of the country. On September 24, with 160,000 Soviet soldiers marshaled on Estonia's frontier, Stalin demanded that Soviet troops be stationed on Estonian territory. Tiny Estonia accepted the demand on the 28th. Poland surrendered to Hitler and Stalin that same day. On October 9, Hitler issued a formal offer. Germany would evacuate all people of German origin from Estonia, Latvia, Lithuania, Eastern Poland and other Eastern provinces. A Baltic German newspaper of that date carried an article quoting Hitler's communiqué. "The *Reval News* reports that 'the Führer of Greater Germany has summoned Baltic Germans in Estonia and Latvia to the fulfillment of new missions.' "

Hitler's communiqué hid the fact that he was secretly permitting Stalin to seize Estonia and the other eastern countries. But events were writing this unmistakable story. My parents were now between a rock and no place at all. The Russians were arriving with an army. My father's noble birth in what had been Czarist Russia and his service against Soviet revolutionaries in 1919 placed him under a formal sentence of death, either as a titled class enemy or as a counter revolutionary. Even twenty years later, deportation to Siberia was certain. He could even be shot. Still, my parents and Grandmama wavered. I heard some of this discussion. They had rebuilt so much, and Estonia was their homeland

A phone call from an English friend, Charles Harwood, proved the deciding event. Knowing of my parents' uncertainty, he called with a blunt warning, practically an ultimatum. As my father later recalled, Harwood had said: "You must be totally mad and been left of your senses. Don't you see the game that is being played here? Hitler has sold the Baltics out to Stalin. The Red Army will march into Estonia within weeks, and I don't have to tell you again that that will be the end of you, me and all of us."

Before saying a hasty good-bye, he told my father that he and his wife were leaving on the next ship to Stockholm. I witnessed this conversation. When Father hung up, he squared his shoulders and stood very upright by the phone. Then he said, "We have to get ready to leave."

The call launched a pandemonium of arrangements, hasty trips to Tallinn, document collection and packing. Of this final month, I have but two memories.

One was my horrid grief when I was told that Tatchen, my beloved nursemaid, had decided not to come with us. Her bags with most of what she owned, including her favorite knick-knacks, were packed. Father had gotten her a passport. But at the last minute, Tatchen had been persuaded by her Estonian relatives to stay. By now she had accumulated considerable savings, and my parents felt that Tatchen's kin did not want to see her money vanish with her overnight. Sometime after the war, we heard that Tatchen had indeed been robbed and later died in misery.

The second memory was from a few days before we left. My father brought me to the front of the house and pointed beyond the tree tops to a line of big ships anchored far off and out to sea.

"Look," he said. "One of those ships will soon take us to a new place, wherever that will be. Oma, Mutti, Ulf and you will leave first. I'll join you later and bring Achti if I can. But before that, there's still lots to be done here."

My earliest memories of Solitude are from the greenhouse. My father specialized in exotic cacti, cyclamen, and tomatoes. His pink and white cyclamen were much prized as Christmas plants in Tallinn, where the long winter nights lent flowers a special power. But it was his hothouse tomatoes in early summer that gave him celebrity status with the nickname *Tomaten Baron* (Tomato Baron.)

I remember the comforting feeling of inclusion while watching my parents work side-by-side repotting the tiny tomato seedlings. My mother's earrings dangled when she lifted me up to the potting table. Then I sat cross-legged near them doing my own stuff—filling and emptying little clay pots with sand. My beautiful, withdrawn mother was always happy when she could work with plants and be together with my father, away from Grandmama and the help. Lost in her own thoughts, she never seemed to notice the sand that I got into my hair and the pockets of my jacket.

My father, a small-boned man with delphinium blue eyes and graceful movements, worked in different versions of the same beige Bermuda-length shorts. In the summer as a protection he wore a white handkerchief on his bald head. For it to stay in place he knotted all corners. I still hear my mother's sparkling voice reminding him to take off "that silly thing" before greeting visitors. When my father took a break, he reached for a wooden box filled with his favorite Egyptian tobacco and Russian paper casings with long mouthpieces. Fascinated, I watched him deftly stuff the *papyrosis* and anticipated the next step, which was for my entertainment only. With a mysterious smile on his suntanned face, he blew pretty blue smoke circles into the air. Sheer magic! How in the world could he do this?

Not so magical, but equally memorable, was the experience of being woken one night, when I was probably around four. My mother carried me in my flannel nightgown to the greenhouse, promising a surprise. There, by the eerie light of the kerosene lamp, my father was puffing his blue rings into the air—and motioning at a cactus.

"Look! Look!" He was in a great state of excitement. "You might not see this ever again. The Queen of the Night! Isn't she lovely?"

I peered dutifully at the sinister whiteness of a large aster-like flower sprouting from a large cactus. Father explained that the blossom appears only one night each year and then for only a few hours. The "queen's" botanical name, he said, was *Cereus*, derived from the Greek *cera*, an allusion to the image of a torch. "You must smell her," he urged. "Her fragrance...exotic...wonderful."

I thought the "queen" smelled awful. All I wanted was to get back to my bed.

My parents owned a single greenhouse when I was born in 1931, but my father, a passionate plantsman, also had a good sense for business. The greenhouse had doubled in size at the time I was shown the *Cereus*. By 1939 my parents were growing their tomatoes, cyclamens and cacti in four greenhouses. The vegetable garden produced asparagus and pole beans. The staff included our handyman Johannes, apprentice gardeners as interns and seasonal part-time

The greenhouses and Aunts' Tower at Solitude, 1930s.

help. This varying cast, along with the household cook and maid, provided most of my companionship. We were more than a mile and a half from any other family. My brother Ulf, three years older than I, was my only playmate. I played with his antique tin soldiers and he played with my Victorian doll. The Napoleonic tin soldiers contained three whole armies—French, Russian and German infantry and cavalrymen. I lined up all the foot soldiers, then brought in the cavalry to topple them regardless of nationality.

The china doll had belonged to my maternal grandmother. But since I was not interested in dolls, Ulf was happy to make her his own. He spent hours dressing and undressing. Her Victorian wardrobe consisted of everything from a whale-boned corset to a burgundy taffeta ball gown with matching feather hat.

When Ulf was six years old, my parents decided to hire a tutor. I do not remember her, but Ulf recalled that she was a friend of Grandmama's. Two years later, to my horror, Ulf was sent away, first to a relative's house, and then to the family of a Lutheran minister in Nõmme, a suburb of Tallinn. The separation caused his gradual estrangement from my parents that lasted to the end of their lives.

I pressed my mother years afterwards to explain why she sentenced Ulf to so hated an exile.

"Ulf was a difficult child," she said. "He wasn't interested in learning his letters. It was even worse with the numbers. The tutor felt Ulf was lazy, stupid or both. I knew better than that, and hoped things would work out gradually. But the tutor lost patience. She believed in physical punishment. She beat Ulf badly. I cried when I heard his screams. Finally I asked Paps to let her go. When Ulf went away, I feared that we might lose him forever. But education is so vital. What were we to do?"

Ulf came home only for summer vacations and at Christmas time. Having been apart for so long, we did not know how to act with each other. I was happy to have him home, but at the same time unhappy with his new personality.

One summer, Ulf had an idea. He wanted to build a castle in the sky, and chose the tallest pine for his site. He never got beyond constructing a platform out of scrap lumber, which he found washed ashore after a storm. The platform, just big enough for two, was wedged between branches high up, hiding it completely from anybody's view.

According to Uncle Carl's book, *Children by the Sea*, Ulf called his castle *Karthago*, after the legendary Phoenician city in North Africa that was conquered by Rome in the Punic Wars. I can't remember that the actual tree house ever had a name. But Ulf rigged up a pulley system with a basket at the end of the rope. We pinched green apples and relished their unripe sourness. There was one catch. I could only reach the castle by pulling myself up with the help of two low branches. For days, we played peacefully, climbing up and down and eating snitched tomatoes and green apples. Then we had an argument. I can't remember why.

"You can't come up here anymore," Ulf said. "It's my castle!"

The next day he sawed off the two branches. I sought refuge in the niche behind my friend Pasha, the stuffed grizzly bear in the hallway. Pasha had been shot by my grandfather. To the bear I complained bitterly, since my mother wouldn't take sides. Life was so unfair. I wanted Ulf to get punished. Punished severely and for life. But Pasha just stood there, a rustic staff held in his mighty paw.

"I'll help you build your own treehouse in that maple over there," my mother consoled. We put up a few boards. But Ulf didn't care about my maple. So neither did I.

According to Uncle Carl's book, Ulf was supposed to be my best friend. But I loved Tatchen more than anybody else. Uncle Carl didn't mention Tatchen at all. She started work for Grandmama as her first lady's maid, when both were about the same age, during the grand times before the Russian Revolution. Tatchen adored me like her own child. Yet because of her age, Tatchen raised me more like a grandmother would. She had few rules. When my parents were away, Tatchen let me eat with her in the kitchen. It was always warm and cozy with Mari, the cook, and Elli, the housemaid, laughing and joking around. They called me *"piima vasikas"* ("little milk calf" in Estonian) for the way I slurped up the milk still foamy and warm from our one cow. Sometimes she let me perch on the big kitchen table, eyes level with her, dangling my feet over the edge. Tatchen didn't make me finish what was on my plate, yet always let me have dessert. Tatchen never made me sit straight on a chair.

Tatchen also took Ulf and me on long walks on our mile of empty beach when we were small. We never went to the right. There, a steep and rocky cliff cut directly into the sea. Turning left, each excursion, especially after a storm, brought something interesting. There were strips of newly washed-up seaweed, sometimes mixed with a glass bottle or pieces of fish netting with cork floats. If we were lucky, we found pieces of amber, the fossilized pine resin found in Europe only along the Baltic Sea. My mother's favorite jewelry was a large, dark, honey-colored amber pendant with an imbedded prehistoric fly in the middle.

I loved to chase the seagulls and sandpipers patrolling the shore. Tatchen tirelessly pointed out for us each familiar boulder thrusting from the sand or the rocky blue-green water. Some were six feet high and had their own names, like the Dromedary, the Hunchback, and the Sphinx. We never tired of climbing and re-climbing them.

I visited Tatchen in her room. Books, boxes, magazines, old letters and documents were stacked in disorderly columns from the floor. China and glass knickknacks filled entire shelves. So much to see, explore. And I was allowed to touch everything. I loved the white porcelain cat with a hole in its back for flowers. Also a set of little mocha cups and saucers ringed in gold and painted with rosy-red roses inside. Then, one day I did the unimaginable. I dropped a favorite—a tiny Dachshund blown out of glass. At the sight of the broken pieces, we both burst out in tears.

"*Gottchen, ach Gottchen!*" ("dear, oh dear") she wailed.

She pressed me to her balcony bosom and wiped both of our eyes with a corner of her apron. For the first time I noticed two long hairs sprouting from a black mole on her chin.

As a surprise present for Easter, my parents gave me a pair of bantam chickens. I named the docile hen Babette and carried her tucked under my arm like Tatchen carried her purse. The little hen did not seem to mind, until the day that I decided to plant her into a flower bed. The idea came from watching my parents plant flow-ers in a round bed in front of the veranda. They did not pay atten-tion to me until my mother discovered Babette's head sticking out of the soil. I had buried her up to her neck. I honestly cannot re-member my motivation, but it seems to me now that most moth-ers never know that children will do strange things. I was given solitary confinement in the nursery for one day. Only Tatchen was allowed to bring me my meals.

It was also Tatchen, of course, who took me on my obligatory visits to Grandmama's house half a mile away through the woods. Grandmama had called her house Tabu, a most appropriate name. I surely dreaded going there. I remember her as a small erect per-son, running on disapproval. She lived with a cook and house-keeper, and during the summer often had visitors. I was too young to understand why she resented me so much. Grandmama had never cared for my mother either. She had fought my parents' engagement, wanting a more charismatic daughter-in-law. Some of her continuing contempt flowed to us, her grandchildren.

In the winter the snow was too deep for walking anywhere. But occasionally I accompanied Mother in our sleigh to the general store in Keila Joa. I loved those trips, bundled up to my chin and listening to the sleigh bells attached to Silvia's harness. Silvia, the purple-black mare, was our only horse. She shared the small stable with a black and white milk cow and a dozen chickens. Animals quickly learn to benefit from each other's warmth in winter. Much to my delight, all our chickens, including my miniature pair, lined up at night sleeping on the two big animals' backs.

One Friday afternoon my mother realized that we did not have enough kerosene left to make it through the weekend. We had no electricity in Solitude, just as we had no truck or car. On our way back from the store, Silvia trotted briskly down the snow-covered embankment leading to the wooden bridge over our creek. Darkness had fallen early and the mare was eager to get home. Suddenly, something spooked her. Maybe it was the

The author as a four-year-old.

trace that touched her hocks. She lifted her tail, let out a tremendous fart and, out of control, raced into a sharp curve. The lightweight wicker sleigh flipped, spilling everything, including me. My mother held on to the reins and disappeared into the darkness. Bundled up and immobile, I waited in the crystalline silence, listening to my own heartbeat as a pungent odor of oil reached my nose. The two kerosene containers must have spilled. In the hurry of departure, we had forgotten to bring the caps. The storekeeper had used potatoes in lieu of corks. When Mother failed to re-appear, scary tales of the Baba Yaga seized my mind. This horrid witch traveled the world in a ramshackle house mounted on giant chicken feet. Tatchen had often told me that one never knew when Baba Yaga would emerge from the woods and devour you. That's what she did: eat children.

By the time my mother returned with Silvia and the sleigh, I had worked myself into such a state that I was unable to speak. I just grunted.

"I couldn't let go of the reins," Mother explained. "They wrapped themselves around my wrist. It was my weight that finally stopped her." When we arrived home, my father, dressed in his heavy overcoat, was ready to come looking for us.

Shortly after my fifth birthday, I was diagnosed with tuberculosis. The word struck terror to my heart. My father's only brother had died from it when he was fifteen. The family physician, Dr. Hasselblatt, sentenced me to sitting outside every day smothered in blankets.

"The cold, dry winter air will do wonders for you," he said.

Each day afterwards, for hours, I was imprisoned on a wicker lounge in the snow. I grew so bored and unhappy that I tried to strike. When the time for outdoors arrived, I threw myself on the floor and kicked anybody coming close.

"I'd rather have tuberculosis," I screamed.

"You might die if you don't do what Dr. Hasselblatt said," Mother insisted. So, out I went, again and again. It became my first painful lesson in discipline.

To lessen the boredom, mother stuck a birdfeeder on a long pole into a snow bank. Watching the chickadees and finches flit back and forth for a time became a temporarily entertaining game. I invented my own bird family fairy tale with a mother, a father, the many children, and the bad witch. I tried to give them all their own names. But I soon had to give up. They all looked alike. This brought tears of frustration, which froze into tiny crystals on my cheeks.

And there was something else. The talk of dying made me think of all the souls that were supposed to go to heaven. I was told that the soul leaves the body at the moment of death. It emerges with the last breath, having been hidden somewhere in the chest. I was certain that on a hot summer's day I had seen many souls rise into the clouds. My rising souls had flimsy, transparent shapes of different size. The tiny ones must belong to babies and small children. I didn't know then that what I was seeing, lying in a warm meadow, were heat waves rising up from the warm earth. So why was there nobody dying in the cold months? Could it mean that in the winter all souls went to hell?

Somehow the time passed and when spring arrived, Dr. Hasselblatt declared me healthy. But he forbade summer bathing, even wading, in the cold sea water of the Gulf. Another unimaginable, harsh restriction.

My first tutor, Fräulein Schmidt, was recruited from an ad in a German newspaper when I was six years old. My parents were giving home education another try. Fräulein Schmidt, a homely woman in plain dress and short bob, was a foreigner and therefore to me quite exotic. An old wooden school desk with attached seat was installed in the nursery. The slanting top opened to a compartment where I kept my books, slate, chalk, paper and pencils. Every morning, six days a week, Fräulein Schmidt and I worked here together. As a treat, we looked at picture books she had brought from Germany. My afternoons were free.

A few weeks into our first semester, Fräulein Schmidt asked me if I wanted to see her room in the *Tantenturm* (aunts' tower). Construction of this square, two-story wooden guesthouse had just been completed. On the ground floor next to the furnace, which also heated an adjacent greenhouse, lived our handyman, Johannes. Another room, more spacious, was Tatchen's new domain. Steep stairs led up to two more guest rooms, one now occupied by Fräulein Schmidt. In her bare and tidy chamber, I right away noticed a photograph under glass in a round, black frame. It showed the stern face of a man with a square mustache.

"Is this your husband?"

"Oh, no." Fräulein Schmidt was visibly embarrassed. "I'm not married. The picture is of my Führer. His name is Adolf Hitler."

She handed me a little flag with a black swastika in a white circle on a bright red background. I was delighted and remembered to thank her for the present. I kept the little flag among my few most prized possessions, and I packed it first when we were preparing to leave Estonia for good a few years later. After all, I wanted to be prepared when we were to arrive in Hitler's Germany.

Fräulein Schmidt had a gift for choreography, in particular with the arrangement of children's plays. A chance to shine came when we planned a surprise party on Grandmama's 75th birthday in August of 1937. Ulf and I were to perform as Grandmama's beloved terriers, Plisch and Plum. Our dialog discussed the pros and cons of our mistress from her dogs' point of view. For weeks we rehearsed and practiced running on all fours. We also practiced barking and growling, not always an easy thing to do. I loved the running on all fours best. I got so good that I outpaced big brother Ulf. Fräulein Schmidt contrived elaborate dog costumes. The face-masks, from paper maché, provided realistically stiff snouts with shiny black button noses, cutouts for eyes, stand-up ears, and well-toothed mouths with flapping red fabric tongues. I especially liked my tail. Fashioned from a cardboard tube, it stood straight up from my white leggings.

The birthday party gathered at Grandmama's house. As always in the summer, she wore yards of filmy whites, gathered with a belt around a tiny waist. An ever-present broad band of black velvet collected the loose skin around her neck. Ulf and I growled and barked our lines, while trying to appear like Plisch and Plum as closely as we could. We grew hotter and sweatier by the minute. But Grandmama never smiled. She just sat there, impassive.

After the final scene, she tossed us, her dogs, bonbons from a bowl. Ulf and I skittered about the lawn chasing the candies. But Plisch and Plum skittered after us, nipping our heels and stealing our bonbons. The nipping hurt my ankles, but what hurt more was that Grandmama's dogs got more candy than we did. At the sight of this bonbon chase, Grandmama laughed so hard that tears ran down her cheeks.

By the time of Grandmama's party, my father had become a success. As the well-known Tomaten Baron, he also had a reputation as an entertaining host. Friends poured in during the summer—we had rooms in the aunts' tower, and in a large Victorian cottage, the *Löwengrube* (the lion's den) near Grandmama's house. My father's charming manner made him a favorite with the ladies in a neighboring Baltic community. During the endless White Nights in June, my parents didn't think it unusual to row several miles in a wooden boat to attend a picnic. The sun was still up when they returned around midnight.

My parents socialized mainly among the small German ethnic minority. They belonged to the *Ritterschafts Verein* (Baltic Nobles Association) in Tallinn, where, mostly in the winter, they attended parties, concerts and plays. To get to Tallinn, they had Johannes take them to the bus station in Keila Joa. When the snow was too deep for the daily bus to get through, I sometimes did not see Mother or Father for days.

My parents had no interest in politics, and I never heard them even mention Hitler. Horticulture, the weather, science, friends, books and culture were among the boring subjects I heard at the dinner table. They were Estonian citizens, but as former overlords, they couldn't have participated much in the newly independent country's political affairs if they had wanted. In the country at large, a succession of center-left governments had fought off the communists after the First World War and built a successful social democracy. Then in the 1930s, with Josef Stalin arming and launching his purges, the ruling coalition under Konstantin Päts banned free speech, arrested right wing leaders, and adopted other repressive measures which it hoped would appease the mighty revolutionary to the east.

At the time, I was totally unaware of any of this.

My first vague fears of war arrived with a radio. My father brought the battery-operated crystal set home sometime in the summer of 1939. Radios had been available in Estonia for some time, but since we did not have electricity, my father had been content to be without until now. We did have some modern instruments. Father loved his Zeiss microscope and his German camera. And we were among the first in the area to have a private crank-up telephone. When it rang, which was seldom, we all ran to it, sharing a high state of anxiety. Father always answered, while we stood around to catch what was being said.

His new radio assumed pride of place on a small table in the living room. Nobody was allowed to touch it, not even Elli with her dust cloth. It usually took father a while to get any kind of intelligible sound. I quietly stayed close, listening to the static. He twiddled with the dials with one hand and cupped the other around his ear. When that didn't help, he pleaded: "Could you please go somewhere else." He once kicked the table in frustration at the static. I couldn't understand the broadcasts from Germany even when they did come through. But my father's anxiety electrified me, and my mother's nervousness did too.

Ulf and I in November 1939.

My memory of these last months in Solitude is strangely sparse. But I was aware of a mounting threat. The phone rang far more often than before. Father would rush the receiver, and soon be shouting, "Speak louder! I can't hear you."

One or another excited friend was on the line with a new rumor. Morning and night the radio set also crackled out some new report. My parents conferred privately. But I overheard the names of countries like Poland, England, Russia and of people like Stalin, Hitler and Päts. A phone call and then a broadcast on the night of August 23 brought the news that Hitler and Stalin had signed a German-Soviet Union Non-Aggression Pact. That treaty publicly asserted the intentions of both countries to live in peace with each other. This promise of peace may have brought a temporary reprieve to my parents. But I cannot recall personally feeling more settled. The phone kept ringing. Rumors still flew through the air. Then came September 1, and Hitler's attack on Poland.

Long after the war, my father wrote in his memoir that, through all the news and rumors of the summer and fall of 1939, he and other Baltic Germans believed they would somehow be able to remain where they were and at peace in their small and doggedly neutral nation. By then the Baltic Germans who had remained after the revolution had established solid businesses, jobs, professional occupations, schools and other institutions and lived in harmony with their hosts. As Father writes:

> We (Baltic Germans) had many hardships in coming to grips with our new condition in Estonia (after 1919), especially in establishing a practical basis for a future for the coming generation. But we also had a firm will to master the situation and adapt ourselves to the new state. The Estonian leadership, growing more conservative with time, had gradually come to recognize the value of our mutual collaboration. So the outbreak of the Second World War struck us (Baltic Germans) like an annihilating bolt of lightning out of a clear blue sky.

Chapter 3

On November 4, my father came to see us off at the gang-plank leading to a German cruise ship docked in the harbor of Tallinn. He was staying behind. The family furniture, library and Grandmama's art collection still had to be crated. He also needed to tie up last-minute negotiations with the Estonian Department of the Interior. The Department was receiving Solitude in a trust settlement. There was a chance that my father could at some future date return and reclaim ownership.

As I held onto my mother's hand, I hummed with excitement about my first excursion on a boat. The weight of my rucksack, which I had packed by myself, reinforced my joy. I was going to go places. The size of the *Ozeana* was far beyond my wildest dreams. She was one of many liners built for *Kraft durch Freude* (Strength through Joy). They were originally used as pleasure ships for German workers and their families. The *Ozeana* was big and beautiful, and black smoke billowed out of her raked chimney. Sailors in white uniforms lined the deck.

My beloved Tatchen and Solitude had vanished from my thoughts. Mother and Grandmama were dressed in their best travel clothes. Grandmama wore her serious black great coat, the inside and collar trimmed in rich sable. On her head she sported a matching *Ushanka*, the typical Russian fur hat with ear flaps tied over the crown. Mother looked elegant in a Tyrolean hat, dark-green velour with trembling pheasant tail feathers fastened to one side. As an about to be eight-year-old, I had no idea of the gravity of the situation or the desperation of my parents. Seven centuries of German and Estonian cohabitation were coming to an end. But I only felt elation.

Walking up the gangplank, I triumphantly turned to wave to my father for the last time. I saw him from a seagull's eye view standing in a group on the dock. My mother's Irish setter, Achti, straining on Father's leash, was barking as my father mouthed some words of farewell. They were lost in the noise from loudspeakers screaming instructions to the passengers.

We gave our names to the officer on deck, who without ceremony crossed them off a long list he was holding in his hand. Another officer assigned us to our cabins. Ulf and I immediately had a fight about who would sleep on the upper berth of the double-decker bed. As always, he won, then triumphantly occupied his lofty kingdom for one night. I heard the ship's whistle, looked out of the small porthole and saw us moving out to sea. Tallinn's landmark churches and 14th century cathedral with its collection of magnificent coats of arms (our own in blue and silver was there) stood silhouetted against the fading sky.

In the evening, everyone gathered in the dining room. *Haken-kreuzfahnen* (swastika flags) hung everywhere, and a photograph of Adolf Hitler was prominently placed above the lavish smorgasbord table. Small round tables were dressed with starched white tablecloths. In the middle of each was a glass vase filled not with flowers but with little paper swastika flags. I thought them just as adorable as the little flag Fräulein Schmidt had given me in Solitude. I wondered if I could take them back to my cabin with me but then thought better of it, knowing that my mother would not approve. A steward, dressed in white, helped us find a table.

Ulf and I had never seen such plentitudes of exotic foods— smoked salmon, ham, herring in sour cream, pickles, thick slices of sourdough bread, and bananas. Imagine, bananas! I thought that we must be coming to the land of milk and honey. How could it get any better than this? Never mind that the adults felt differently.

"*Ach, wäre ich doch wieder zu Hause* (Oh, to be back home)," Grandmama sighed as she looked at her untouched food. She said it again and again, while Ulf and I demolished our suppers. My mother had not even joined us. She had come down with a migraine and stayed in her cabin with a silk bandana wrapped around her forehead.

During the night, the *Ozeana* encountered rough seas. The pitching and rolling of the ship caused our stomachs to reject the rich food we had so much enjoyed the night before. Early next morning, our steward came in to bring fresh towels and hot water. His eyes opened wide at what he saw.

"Oh, shit." He quickly slammed the door. I felt bad about the mess but was shocked at his profanity.

Later that morning, the loudspeaker announced to get ready for docking. By now we had left the open sea and were steaming up the broad mouth of the Oder River. My mother had appeared on deck to watch the landing in Szczecin. From a distance, I could already see a massing of swastika flags swelling in the November morning air. Welcome banners written in German Gothic swaggered with triumph:

Deutschland Siegt (Germany Conquers)

Grossdeutschland Grüsst Euch (Greater Germany Greets You)

We had arrived in Nazi-occupied Poland, soon to become part of the Third Reich. On shore, loudspeakers competed with the ones on board ship. The noise was ear-shattering. When they suddenly stopped, we could hear music from a marching band assembled on the dock:

Auf der Heide blüht ein kleines Blümelein,

Und es heisst, Erika.

(On the meadow blooms a tiny flower,

And it's called, Erika.)

To my great embarrassment, my mother broke out into tears and rushed back to her cabin. She hated the familiar marching song glorifying her name. She had never liked being a sweet little flower

Nazi Germany welcomes Baltic German evacuees in Szczecin, Poland.

blooming on the heath. Thoughts of Estonia might have played a role too. Grandmama held on to the ship's railing, viewed the scene bleakly and said for everyone to hear: "Oh, to be losing my Estonia."

Despite a well-organized reception, it took hours to get the 836 passengers off the ship and through the preliminary documentation for naturalization. For the first time, I heard us being called *Rückwanderer* (returnees.)

"Returnees to where?" Mother wondered. "It's been centuries since we left Germany."

While we waited, a field kitchen served hot soup and bread in military metal bowls. In the late afternoon we were ordered to board a train, which was to take us overnight to a camp in Poznan in central Poland. The SS had chosen Poznan to be the center of immigration and naturalization for the "returnees" streaming in every day. Heinrich Himmler was in charge. His title for this particular job was *Reichskommissar für die Festigung Deutschen Volkstums* (Reich's Commissioner for the Strengthening of German Nationhood). We were told that in a "returnee" camp we would have an extensive medical examination and then, only if we passed, receive German naturalization. Grandmama heard rumors that we would personally be greeted by Hitler once we got there. It seemed to cheer her up.

The final immigration and naturalization report to Heinrich Himmler counted 61,500 Baltic Germans transferred to Poland in 93 trips by ship: 12,868 immigrated from Estonia; 48,641 from Latvia.

According to an edition of the *Baltische Briefe* (Baltic Letters), published in 1964 and commemorating the 25th anniversary of the evacuation of the Baltic Germans, Hitler in 1939 had said that he valued Baltic German commoners but "had no use for the morbid Baltic aristocrats." Yet we von Bremens and others had qualified anyway. The SS report to Himmler found the "racial purity" of all the Baltic Germans noteworthy.

In early November, the Nazis established the *Deutsche Umsiedlungs-Treuhandgesellschaft* (German Resettlement Trust Corporation).

This organization, also run by the SS, was under nominal direction of Germany's deputy minister of foreign affairs, Wilhelm Keppler. The real estate and other assets of Baltic German landowners, business establishments and banks were signed over to the German government through this trust. It pretty much covered the costs of evacuation of the "returnees" and committed Germany to pay some form of compensation to the newly arrived citizens for their losses. Politically, Hitler sought to hide the fact that he was arranging a more or less forced evacuation of refugees from countries he had turned over to Stalin. Hence the label "returnees" that was applied to us. Hence also the official German government statement announcing the proposed evacuation in Estonia and Latvia. It applied an upbeat spin to a withdrawal. The statement's key wording: "The Fuhrer has called the Baltic Germans back from their centuries-old posts defending German interests to assign them new tasks. He is, therefore, giving them a new homeland."

It sounded as if we had all voluntarily left our homes and fortunes in Estonia and Latvia to seek this promising new land. Some had done so. Committees of willing Baltic Germans in Estonia had quickly been formed to promote and help manage the evacuation. But for others, and especially my parents, the evacuation was pure flight, an escape from a darker fate.

The train trip to Poznan took us through a black and moonless night. I remember being cold in the unheated compartments but tried to be a brave eight-year-old and not complain. There were many unexplained stops, often preceded by shots—gunfire!—at which everyone woke up with a start.

"What's happening? Where are we now?"

One rumor sweeping the train had it that the stops were caused by Polish-laid mines that had to be removed from the rails. The shootings were rumored to come from Polish guerillas. Reflecting on it much later as an adult, I believe some of the gunfire could also have come from German evacuation squads forcing Polish civilians from their homes.

Evidence of the *Blitzkrieg's* devastation was everywhere along the tracks as dawn unfolded. From the train windows I could see houses with shot-out windows and broken walls and the charred remnants of farm buildings. I spotted small plots with freshly dug graves. Crude wooden crosses marked the mounds. All the previous excitement that I had felt before had now evaporated in the stale and frigid air of the compartment. I had become immobilized with a deep depression about the uncertainty of events to come. I imagine I must have been embarrassed to ask questions to which nobody could give me any answers.

We arrived in Poznan bleary-eyed from lack of sleep. I was disappointed that there was no band greeting us at the train station. Grandmama was disappointed that Hitler was not there personally greeting us as had been rumored. She was still numb with grief. "Oh, to be losing my Estonia," she said again.

Struggling out of the station, we climbed unceremoniously into open German military trucks, which jolted us to a school in the outskirts of the city. Our group of four, together with twelve other refugees, were assigned a small classroom. It had been emptied of all desks and chairs. Piles of loose straw lined the walls instead. One wall had a map of Poland on which somebody had scribbled many black swastikas. A single table and one straight chair stood in the middle of the room. Underneath the table was a chamber pot. This particular school had no indoor plumbing. A cold-water pump in the small washroom served us all, and a muddy path led to four ramshackle wooden outhouses a short distance behind the school.

I wondered what had happened to all the students. I felt relieved not to be faced by them. It dawned on me for the first time that soon I would have to go to a real school. No more tutors. I felt unsure of myself and worried about how I'd behave in the presence of many strange children. What language would they speak? Would they be hostile towards me? These thoughts and fears were more troubling than the gunfire I'd heard and the graves I'd seen.

"I don't think that I can sleep here," Grandmama said, sitting down on the only chair when everyone was staking out a place on the straw. "Erika, why don't you tell the official that your seventy-seven-year-old mother-in-law cannot sleep on the floor."

Mother did not look at Grandmama. "I'm getting a migraine," she said, "and I better lie down."

When Grandmama found out that nobody paid attention to her, she reluctantly squeezed in between my mother and me. Later that night, we found our way in the dark to an unlit outhouse. Again we stood in line, shivered in our nightclothes and listened to distant gunshots. Back on the floor, we covered ourselves with gray military blankets handed to us and tried to get to sleep.

I wondered about unhappy, imperious Grandmama. What a change for her! What was going through her mind, lying motionless with closed eyes next to me? I couldn't imagine her thoughts then. And it is something that I will never know. I was always too scared of her to ask.

My grandmother was born into privilege and married even more of it. At the age of twenty-one, on November 18, 1883, Maria Stella Countess Rehbinder married a nobleman seven years her senior, Constantin von Bremen. The arranged wedding took place in the ancestral mansion of her father, the old Count Reinhold Rehbinder of Udriku about sixty miles southeast of Tallinn. The ceremony consummated a classic feudal union. It joined the extensive holdings of the Rehbinders to the renown of a particularly ancient family, the von Bremens. The first von Bremen arrived in pagan Estonia from Germany with the original Christian Crusaders, the Brotherhood of the Sword, in the early 13th century. This was the Baltic German equivalent of an American's forebearers arriving on the Mayflower. A giant tombstone of a von Bremen who died in 1388 is displayed to this day on a wall in the Katariina Passage in the old city of Tallinn.

At the time of my grandparents' wedding, Estonia's peasants

were nominally free—official serfdom had ended in 1816. A national awakening to rouse and educate a largely illiterate native Estonian population had begun thirty years later. But even so, in 1883, a basic feudal system still prevailed. Except in a handful of cities, 95 percent of the population had no vote or role in government. A Senate of Baltic German nobles and representatives of the biggest cities ran national, provincial and local affairs under the loose sovereignty and protection of the Russian czar. The German overlords, like the Count Rehbinders and von Bremens, still owned most of the farmland and forests. Estonian citizens and peasants, though legally free, remained prevented by law from buying any of the noble lands. The law required peasants instead to provide physical labor to the local noblemen as rental payment on the plots granted them for private cultivation. Thus a form of labor bondage still endured. Some judicial power even remained with the local lord. My grandfather held court as justice of the peace over affairs occurring within his own estate. The Baltic Germans spoke German as their first language, Russian as their second, and Estonian as their third. A sort of colonialism as well as feudalism prevailed.

The wedding couple doubtless made a dazzling pair as they descended the broad staircase at Udriku that November day in 1883. The mansion, with neo-classic limestone exterior, columned porticoes, eighteen-foot interior ceilings, ballroom, drawing rooms, music room and dozens of other chambers, still survives. So does its surrounding English-style park. The estate now serves as an Estonian insane asylum.

The wedding guests would have numbered in the hundreds. But Grandmama's mother, Ernestine Baroness von Ungern Sternberg, did not attend. When Grandmama was only five, amid great scandal, her mother had run away to Italy from what she felt to be a stifling marriage and the harsh Estonian climate. It was whispered in Estonian society, I much later learned, that she had entered a common law relationship with an Italian aristocrat and had borne two more children. By the time of her wedding, Grandmama had made sure that the mention of Ernestine was taboo. It stayed that way to her death. When I was in my late twenties, I raised the subject with my father for the first and what turned out to be the last time.

Father was normally open-minded. But not now.

"That grandmother," he snapped, "was not supposed to exist. I can't tell you anything about her." He looked at me for a moment longer, his eyes asking if we understood each other. I will not ask that question again soon, I thought.

Growing up as the only woman in a large house, Grandmama became the apple of her father's eye. She was deprived of nothing, enjoyed the best of private tutoring, and at an early age became her father's companion and hostess. She embraced life with the confident impulsiveness possible only to someone born into the ruling class. She ran a large household staff of servants, including the first butler, the chief cook, and head coachman. There was also her father's *valet de chambre*, a footman, and her own lady's maid, Berta. (Berta was later to become my nursemaid and be nicknamed Tatchen.) She addressed Grandmama as *Gnädige Frau* (My Lady) from the moment she was hired, even though both of them were young women of about the same age. By the time Grandmama was eighteen, she was fluent in Estonian, Russian and French along with her first language, German. She never desired to learn English, believing it the language of commerce—not style.

"It is a pity that you never knew your grandfather," Grandmama often said. "He was the most wonderful person...but most of all, he adored me and I adored him."

Their companionship and her duties instilled an assertiveness and self-confidence in Grandmama which the average nobleman of the era would have instilled only in a firstborn son.

My grandparents set off on their 1883 honeymoon in late November, traveling by train, coach and ultimately by ferry to Sicily. Italy and the Riviera were the standard wintering places for nobles of the North. But my grandparents were hardly standard. Costi, as

Grandmama called her husband, was considerably taller than Grand-mama, sported an impressive mustache, and was partial to wearing white suits. A gold watch would have been tucked into his waistcoat pocket, at the end of a double loop of heavy gold chain.

"A section of it was later made into a necklace," my father later said. "It was my wedding present to Mutti." When my mother died, the necklace was passed on to me. The necklace and a silver candle-snuffer are the only belongings of my grandfather that have survived.

Grandmama was a small woman with an hourglass figure, a mass of iridescent black hair (she called them "pig bristles") and blue, heavily lidded eyes. She dressed as she liked, often favoring her riding habit. My grandparents took no servants to Sicily. Theirs was a tour to explore each other amid the romance of art, antiqui-ties, and golden weather.

In these days of easy travel, it is hard to imagine the delight that filled the hearts of the few rich northern Europeans who were lucky enough to travel south in the 18th and 19th centuries. Grand-mama often quoted Goethe from his *Italian Journey, 1786 – 1788:* "Without Sicily, Italy leaves no image in the soul. Sicily is the key to everything."

In a letter to her brother, Heinrich, she cited these lines from a favorite Goethe poem:

> Knowst thou the land where the citrons bloom,
> Where golden oranges gleam in the dark leaves,
> Gentle breezes blow from the blue sky,
> And the calm myrtle and tall laurels grow?
> Dost thou know it?
> There, there,
> Oh my beloved, I long to go with thee.

In another letter to Heinrich she wrote:

> In Palermo we roomed at the comfortable Palazzo In-gham. We were privileged to see the extraordinary mosaics

in the Palatine Chapel of the Norman Palace. I saw no place so small yet had so much to show in mosaics and *piètre dure* stone work…but it was in Syracuse that I lost my heart to a sheep. Yes, a sculpture of a reclining ram with magnificent spiral horns.

Goethe, in his own journals, had mentioned two of these larger-than-life-sized, third century B.C. Greek bronzes. He wrote that the recumbent rams guarded the entrance to the ruins of the Hellenic Maniace Fortress, which had protected Syracuse before it fell to Rome. By the time my grandparents discovered it, only one remained. Museum catalogues from 1883 report that it was then on display at a Syracuse museum. Now the ram is well displayed in the Regional Archeological Museum of Palermo.

Grandmama, however, had created her own story. "One day Grandpapá and I came upon an archeological dig, and just by chance, we witnessed the ram being freed from the rubble."

Grandmama had a piètre dure three-quarter-sized copy of the ram cast, then shipped it back to Avanduse. "Sicily is just a heav-

Grandmama in Avanduse with paintings and copy of the Greek bronze ram.

enly place," she told and retold me as a child. "Antiquities were every-where, strewn on the ground among the grazing sheep."

When spring came to Sicily, the newlyweds were dazzled by the thousands of new blossoms opening each day. First to bloom was the ancient almond, symbol of hope to Greeks and newlyweds. Pale pink clouds of these flowering trees graced the valleys and matched the pink of snow-cover on Mt. Etna at sunset. The countryside was thick with wildflowers. Orange calendula, white chamomile, swaths of lemon yellow wood sorrel and lavender pools of crocus flowed through the orchards. Reveling in the honeyed perfume of the al-mond blossoms, Grandmama felt in paradise.

When the newlyweds returned to Estonia, they first settled in Võivere, an estate Grandmama had inherited from her not-to-be-mentioned mother. Thirteen years later, in 1896, Grandfather ac-ceded to Avanduse, an uncommonly large property close to the eastern virgin forests.

Avanduse brought the land he owned in various estates to 27 square miles. Avanduse alone included two manor houses and three villages, Poidifer, Venevere and Simuna. The inheritance came from my grandfather's older brother Karl, who had died young when still a bachelor. Avanduse and the attached village of Simuna were as self-contained as a small town. Several hundred families lived in the vicinity containing the estate's distillery, its fish ponds, a carpenter and cabinet maker's shop, a forge and smithy, a store, a road house, saw mills, warehouses, extensive stables for horses, hothouses, a school, a church and graveyard.

The estate had fallen into neglect, but Grandpapa saw the pos-sibility of great riches. He now held as much land as almost anyone in Estonia. The timber alone was a potential gold mine. Under his careful management, that is what it became.

In his memoirs, my father wrote:

> Papá was an astute and innovative businessman his whole life. He installed an electric generator, and had elec-tric lights and power at Avanduse, for instance, half a dozen

years before electricity arrived in Tallinn, the nation's capital.

Mamá went to work on her own dream. She hired Rudolph von Engelhardt, a St. Petersburg architect familiar with the villas of Andrea Palladio (1505-1580.) Even Goethe had been enthralled: "There is something divine about his (Palladio's) talent, something comparable to the power of a great poet, who out of the world of truth and falsehood, creates a third whose borrowed existence enchants us."

Engelhardt carried through Mamá's plan to connect the two 18th-century country houses with a round-arched conservatory. Palm trees later over-wintered there and shaded a painter's easel Grandmama used for her oil paintings.

Grand Palladian windows, nearly floor to ceiling, and double glazed against the northern cold, were sunk into the facades of the buildings themselves, replacing smaller openings. As Father noted:

> For the interior, Mamá picked contemporary motifs, a blend of pre-Raphaelite and Arts and Crafts. She made sure that every piece of basic interior decoration, from limestone fireplaces, mantels and torchieres to tapestries, wallpaper and wood paneling, was handcrafted on the premises. So were the giant frames of the Palladian windows themselves. They were built locally from drawings Mamá had made of Palladian window designs.

Grandmama had taken art lessons in the studios of painters in Italy before her marriage. She designed the motifs for the carved plaster moldings and ceilings, then painted the friezes atop Avanduse's seventeen-foot-high grand hall walls herself.

From my father's diary:

> This unseemly manual act by a countess outraged local gossip. One day Reverend Paukker, pastor of our church in Simuna, came by for an official visit. Dressed formally in his black frock coat and trousers, holding his black hat, he was

shown to the grand hall. There was Mamá, perched on scaffolding, dressed in men's pants and splattered painter's frock. Dumfounded and without uttering a single word he took flight. The story of his shock circulated within days to every villager. Pastor Paukker required weeks to compose himself before returning to complete his business with Mamá.

Visitors who arrived by carriage or on horseback approached Avanduse by a circular driveway leading to the buttery yellow Palladian portico. A butler invited the visitor to the bright vestibule. Once entered, the visitor was surprised by the sight of an imposing stuffed bear.

"It was killed by my grandfather in self defense," my father told me. "He was out hunting on foot with a game warden when the hounds roused a bear. Grandpapá shot him with his revolver just seconds before he was upon him."

The bear was typical of Grandmama as an art collector in one specific. Hers was a personal aesthetic. She chose art and artifacts that made reference to her own travels and experiences, her understanding of history, her spiritual feelings, or her lifestyle. Totally

Avanduse in spring 1900.

self-confident, she assumed that great art simply had to be whatever she liked.

"She proudly displayed everything, ranging from the castings of the third-century B.C. Greek sheep, to an oil of the Doges Palace in Venice, to an Anthony van Dyke Crucifixion, to original Greek marbles, on to exquisite watercolors of the ruins in Rome. She had an almost obsessive passion for horses—riding and hunting and breeding better horses for work and pleasure on the estate. She rode only in sidesaddle, where she sat her horse like a general. She collected countless equine images, from antique stone friezes to the

Grandmama always rode in a side saddle.

oils of Christian Speyer (1855 to 1929), a then-famous German romantic horse painter. Included in the Speyer collection was a magnificent 12-foot-by-6-foot triptych, "The Apocalypse." The large central section pictured a dark and stormy sky through which the four horsemen galloped airborne above a landscape with villages below. The stallions were painted slightly from behind, emphasizing their powerful hindquarters, flying tails, visible anuses and swinging genitals. Energy! The dramatic, sexy central canvas was flanked by two narrower panels depicting white rearing stallions. Desperately clinging to each horse was, respectively, a male and female nude.

Grandmama also searched the galleries of European museums and private collections she visited for portraits capturing expressions she remembered on a loved one's face. She usually found these fleeting smiles, moments of anger, or self-assurance in works of old masters in museums. Since she could not buy them, she simply commissioned copies of them all.

The long, cold and restless first night on the school floor in Poznan, Poland, finally passed. Grandmama, Mother and I were woken by a shout from the ever-present loudspeaker. Everyone had slept so close together that we looked like a can of sardines coming to life. A penetrating voice told us about the schedule of the day: breakfast first, then a line-up for a medical examination in the gymnasium. Female "returnees" and their small children were to line up separately from their male relatives. Ulf was found to be too old to come with us. As an eleven-year-old, he bravely joined the group of strange men in another room.

Amid this confusion I saw, for the first time, Grandmama and my mother in their underwear. We disrobed before a German doctor conducting the medical examination. Mother had barely been able to move from her bed of straw, but now stood bravely in line, just like everybody else, except that she still had a silk bandana wrapped around her forehead.

But Grandmama's underwear was most interesting. I was seeing a part of her that I felt I was not supposed to see. I could not help looking. It came in two parts—a chemise and the *pantalon de femme*, which reached below her knee and was finished with a lacy ruffle. The two legs of her underpants were separate, held together only by a drawstring at her waist. Studying the construction of Grandmama's underwear, I came to the conclusion that her drawers were far superior to the cotton tricot underpants I was wearing, at least for the purpose of visiting the cold and messy outhouse.

The doctor, in a white coat, was a burly man who kept his arms away from his body as if they hurt from a sunburn. His forehead glistened in a film of sweat. First he listened to the chest, he felt the pulse and finally looked down our throats. Then he had questions. Most of them centered on our ancestry and if there were any *Erbkrankheiten* (hereditary diseases) in the family. My mother answered patiently despite her throbbing headache.

"We are descendents of Teutonic knights who came to Estonia in the 13th century. There was never any intermarriage with gypsies, Jews or Negroes. We have no hereditary diseases. You can see for yourself how healthy my seventy-seven-year-old mother-in-law is." A nurse wearing a Red Cross uniform gravely recorded her answers.

When it was Grandmama's turn, she asked why a seventy-seven-year-old lady was not provided with a bed. The doctor replied with a wave that in due time she might get a bed to sleep in, but he could not promise when that was going to be. *"Wie schön war es doch in der Heimat"* (It was so beautiful back home), she sighed.

A few mornings later, I woke up with a piercing pain in my left ear. My burning hot face indicated an elevated temperature. The same burly German doctor who had examined us days before diagnosed an acute middle ear infection.

"This child will have to be hospitalized right away. I cannot treat her here," he said.

My mother had recovered from her migraine. She located a

nearby street car that took us to the suggested Polish hospital in the center of Poznan.

It took a while to get me admitted. The woman behind the desk only spoke Polish. The pain in my ear became so excruciating that all I could do was throw myself on the floor and scream as loudly as I could. Quickly, it brought a reaction. A German military doctor accompanied by a Polish nun entered the scene. They lifted me off the floor and walked me upstairs to a large hall filled with beds. I don't remember much of what happened next, but I know that the following day the pain had ceased considerably. I was now well enough to see that I was the only child in a hall of female patients. Only a few spoke or wanted to speak German, and since nobody seemed interested in me, I was left pretty much alone. This gave me time to contemplate the only picture on the wall, a larger-than-life image of Christ, hanging over the door. He wore a crown of thorns, his painful gaze lifted upwards. Big drops of blood trickled down his pale face.

Polish nuns belonging to the Order of the Sisters of Charity of St. Vincent de Paul looked after me. They were dressed in long black and white habits and wore winged hoods on their heads. The stiffly starched hoods stuck out so far that the only way for the nuns to pass through a door was to go sideways.

When I was well enough to walk about, I was told that I could check the waiting hall downstairs to see if my mother had come during visiting hours in the afternoon. She had just arrived when I found her there the next day. Her hugs and kisses did not come too soon. I had felt terribly abandoned.

"I'm bringing you good news. The doctor said that in a few days you might be able to leave the hospital. He put in a special request for better housing. It should mean a bed for Oma, a warm room for you and a solid roof over our heads when Paps comes in a couple of weeks."

When I returned to my hospital room, I was surprised to find one of the younger patients sitting on my bed. She was holding a shoebox on her lap.

"It took me a while to get all this together, but now that it's done, the moment is here for you to take the box to my fiancé," she said.

By "fiancé" she meant a German officer, recovering from his wounds in the men's section of the hospital. Women were not permitted to enter there, but the young woman figured that a child would not be stopped. She pressed the open shoebox into my hands. Inside, dressed like a bride in surgical gauze, was a fresh herring. The pointy mouth and bulging eyes were all that was visible in the bridal veil. Tucked into the side was a sealed envelope with the name of the officer, Lt. Peter Schönecker, written on the front.

"Now you go and deliver this box to the lieutenant in room number 5. I'll wait right here until you get back."

I felt important but also a little embarrassed to be asked on such an unusual mission. I thought that a herring, dressed like a bride in a shoebox, was very bizarre. At the same time, I was scared knowing that what I was asked to do did not comply with hospital rules. I must have run all the way to the third floor, because when I knocked on room No. 5, I was breathless. I meant to say that I had a message, but I could not say the words. The officer, whose head and face were partially obscured by a huge bandage, opened the box and read the note.

"Oh, for heaven's sake. She's totally crazy," he laughed. "You go back and tell her what I said."

I ran back hoping not to run into one of the nuns. Who knows what she would have done to me? When I reached my hall, the young woman still sat on my bed. I told her exactly what he had said. Her face changed to such sadness that I thought she would break into tears. Instead, she went back to her bed and pulled the blanket over her head.

My mother came to pick me up a day later. The first snow of the season had fallen during the night. It was cold, but the dreary streets looked lovely and I thought about Christmas.

"We are going to a large villa," she whispered in the crowded street-car. "It belongs to a Polish family who was asked to leave just yesterday. Everybody will have their own bed now. Oma's much happier."

But why was she whispering the good news? The streetcar was crowded with Poles. It took me a long time to understand the reason for this new secrecy.

When my mother unlocked the front door of the villa at *Benschener Strasse,* she tried to suppress a burst of tears.

"What is the matter?" I asked.

"It's all so terrible…" Mother said. "I'm very frightened… I wish Paps was here. The tea on the breakfast table was still hot when I first came with the German official. The family must have just left minutes before." Mother grabbed my arm. "Don't go any further until you hear what I say! This house does not belong to us. The family was forced out. We are only their guests until they return."

What was going on? As an eight-year-old, it was beyond me. I learned only much later that the family whose house we used was among tens of thousands of the Polish elite who were forced from urban homes and country estates in western Poland. The vacant real estate was reassigned to not only Baltic Germans like us but to "returnees" from other regions, such as Galizia, and also to German nationals from Germany looking for new job opportunities. We were to turn this area, the western third of Poland, into the *Warthegau,* a new part of Germany itself. On short notice and mostly during the night, the evicted Polish civilians were taken to camps, then shipped to a newly created General Government sector of German-occupied Poland. This territory comprised the south central Polish provinces of Lubin and parts of Cracow and Warsaw. The seat of the General Government was moved from Warsaw to Cracow. Hans Frank, a Munich Nazi Party leader, installed himself as the new leader in a former royal residence. Frank's reign was one of the most horrible and brutal of all Nazi directorates. Three million Jews and almost as many Poles were murdered in the General Government. Frank was hanged in 1946 after being convicted of war crimes in the Nuremberg Trials.

I was oblivious to these unfurling horrors and very happy in my new house on *Benschener Strasse*. It had many toys—fancy toys I had never seen before. Right away, I became attached to a little red elephant with a movable trunk, fashioned from beads strung on an elastic band. Smitten, I asked if I could keep it. "Absolutely not," my mother said. "The child and the child's family will come back and expect to find everything the way they left it. We all have to see to that." Another fascination was boxes and boxes of paper clips. I spent hours making Christmas gifts of chains and necklaces for Grandmama and my mother.

On December 19, my father arrived just in time for Christmas. He was among 271 others on the next-to-last ship out of Tallinn. The *Orotava,* a small freighter built to transport anything from cattle to bananas, this time had brought only evacuees and a few of their pets. Achti preceded my father through the door, jumped up on my mother and licked her face. Later that night, my parents and Grandmama talked in Russian to each other. They did this when they did not want us kids to understand. My mother cried again, so I knew it had something to do with the Polish villa.

Months later, my mother confided when we were alone in the kitchen that she had asked the Nazi official showing her the house about the fate of the Polish owners. What would they do in the General Government area? The official finally became annoyed. "They will be fine there," he declared. "Don't you worry about them."

Up until we took that house, my parents' feelings about their first weeks in "The Third Reich" had been generally favorable. The forces of order were prevailing, and order is deeply rooted in German nature. My parents were doing as they were told. But now, they had their first inkling about how the Nazi occupation was going to handle the Poles whose properties were of interest to them. My parents seemed to be shocked at the brutal circumstances. And how could they have felt at such propaganda posters as *Wer bei einem Juden kauft is ein Volksverräter* (Buying from a Jew is racial treason)? Yet at the same time, I believe they were like most of the "returnees." Their own survival was in question; self-preservation was fore-most in their minds. Also, my parents had just lost almost every-thing for the second time in their lives. The first blow was the loss of estates and possessions in the Estonian agrarian reforms in the 1920s. Now they were benumbed refugees from Estonia. And there was one more excuse. Most of the Warthegau had belonged to Ger-many before World War I. All these were factors for denial, for sup-pressing open outrage over the plight of other people.

In their own vulnerable state, the Baltic Germans must also have felt overpowered by the Nazi regime's propaganda. Loud-speakers and banners were everywhere. *Ein Volk, ein Reich, ein Führer* (One Race, One Realm, One Leader); *Nationalsozialismus, der Organ-isierte Wille der Nation* (National Socialism, the Organized Will of the Nation). Simultaneously, my parents and other returnees must have visualized new possibilities for a workable and maybe even prof-itable existence. The Nazis had promised to consider the Balts' pre-vious social and economic standing and to match them as closely as possible when assigning seized businesses and assets. In the case of my father, the German resettlement authorities considered him economically elite, valuable because he had the business and agri-cultural knowledge to manage a large farming property.

To begin the task in agriculture, the Nazis asked a few previ-ous Baltic landowners for help in conducting a survey of Polish farms and forest lands. My father, interested in the process, applied at the newly formed German survey organization, called *Ostland* (East Land). Quickly he discovered that the leadership of this or-ganization lay in the hands of two people he knew from Estonia, Helmuth Weiss and a cousin, Erik von Bremen. My father started his new job right after Christmas with the use of a car—an Opel—and driver. He had never learned how to drive a car. All his life he had only been an accomplished equestrian.

All through the winter of 1940, I saw very little of him, but my impression was that he liked his new job. He appreciated look-ing at good soil, though now frozen hard and often under the cover of snow. A passionate farmer, he was able to determine at a glance if a farm was well run or not. He could see it from the state of winter wheat to the existence or availability of farm machinery to the condition of the livestock and horses. He could also see the farm's potential for improvement. Some crops, like sugar beets and wheat, were wasted growing in many of the rich soils. My father called the richest agricultural lands he visited, that were wrongly devoted to beets, *Zuckerrübenwüste* (sugar beet deserts).

When he came upon Majkow, a 540-acre farm with a small estate house, he knew that it was the farm he wanted to manage. His creativity, his love for experimentation and the fact that he was on the cutting edge when it came to vegetable farming are all expressed in this note on the estate in his memoir:

> Majkow has fantastic black soil presently wasted on sugar beets and wheat. Should I be in charge, I would change it to a vegetable truck farm. Tomatoes, cucumbers and green beans by the acres would be possible here. Majkow is very close to the city (Kalisz) and Kalisz is on the main railroad between Posnan and Lódz. I could easily ship tons of tomatoes for canning anyplace connected with that railroad...
>
> When I first saw Majkow, the Polish owner had already left. The dairyman was reluctant to talk but eventually said that the owners were elderly and not in the best of health. Supposedly, they now live in an apartment in Warsaw. Other farm workers were reluctant to talk. They appeared to be worried about what was going to happen. I tried to assure them, that they would be all right if I had anything to do with it. But I'm sure that they did not believe me.

Thinking about this entry in his memoir later, it was clear to me that any feelings of shame had been replaced by a feeling for survival. There is also no doubt that both of my parents and also Grandmama saw a chance to return to a lifestyle of "landed gentry." The golden past of the decades before 1917 might be somewhat recreated right here in Majkow. For my father the thought must have brought back memories of his own glorious years as the heir apparent to Avanduse. At the very least, he could see a quick recovery of his more recent fortunes, this time not just as a *Tomaten Baron* but as a king of all vegetables.

Chapter 4

On a lovely day in the spring of 1940, our family was picked up from the Kalisz railroad station in central Poland by a carriage pulled by a team of two bright bays. A liveried coachman took us in a brisk trot through the center of Kalisz. Most of the city streets had been changed from Polish to German names. We passed city hall, then bounced on cobble-stoned *Hermann Göring Allee* through *Adolf Hitler Platz*. Swastika flags were everywhere.

Achti was between my knees, enjoying the closeness of our bodies. Once we were through town, we continued on dirt roads bordered by fields of green winter wheat. We had become quiet, filled with expectations. My face was flushed with excitement. What was this place called Majkow going to be like?

When we passed the soldiers' cemetery, my father pointed to a stand of large trees in the near distance:

"That's Majkow over there. The trees that you see are of the big park, right behind the house."

When we turned into the circular gravel driveway, I was overwhelmed by the sight of the house, a neo-classical mansion. Achti began wagging her tail. She must have approved of what she saw. The horses pulled up at the front door, which was swung open by two curtsying maids. They stepped up to greet us. My father and Achti led the way inside. He took us on a tour of the house. A few days later, I explored everything else: the stables, the dairy barn, the greenhouse, and the large English-style park. These became my playground for a few years to come.

The garden side of Majkow's manor house.

That fall, as a nine-year-old, I was sent to school for the first time, starting in the third grade of the only German school in Kalisz, the recently renamed *Oberst Mölders Schule*. I had been home tutored in Solitude and was now terrified by the thought of a real school and meeting with real, strange children. Simultaneously, I was dying to make friends and be part of a group of girls. Thinking back now, I consider myself lucky to have made the adjustment from a withdrawn and lonely child as well as I did. It could have been very different. I could have easily become an introvert for life. As it was, I sat mostly in silence through several months of classes, watching the others, then meeting a kindred soul in Paula, another frightened little girl. Soon we were accepted in an expanding circle of playmates. After all my nightmares, it went amazingly easy. I still don't understand why.

My brother Ulf went to the same school. But he demanded that I not embarrass him at recess with references of playing together. I was to stick with the kids from my class. He would stick to his friends from the Gymnasium. "School is different," he said gruffly. "We can still play when we are home. Maybe."

We learned the first day that our school building had been re-

named for German Colonel Werner Mölders, who was commander
of the *Jagdgeschwader* 51 (Fighter Squadron 51), which flew mostly
over France and the English Channel. After downing of his 40th
enemy plane, he had been awarded the *Ritterkreuz mit Eichenlaub*
(Knights Cross with oak leaves.) Also that first day we learned to
greet each teacher by raising our right arms only a little above the
level of our shoulder and simultaneously shouting "*Heil Hitler.*" My
homeroom teacher urged us to *Heil Hitler* when greeting our parents too. Some instinct told me not to try that, ever. By then I knew
that our family was sticking to the handshake in personal greetings.
I still curtsied and kissed Grandmama's hand every morning.

During Monday school assembly in the gymnasium, the rituals
of the new regime were always honored. All students stood and
sang the German national anthem, "*Deutschland, Deutschland über
alles…*" Then, while an upper-class student raised the Nazi flag, we
sang a Nazi song, the *Horst Wessel Lied*: "*Die Fahne hoch, die Reihen fest
geschlossen…*" (The flag held high, our ranks drawn tight together …).
At the end of assembly, the entire student body raised their arms
in unison and shouted "*Heil Hitler*" once again. I was always slow
in catching on to how to do things right in school. Mostly I lacked
the snappiness of raising my arm and keeping a stiff back required
when greeting the raised flag. Above my homeroom teacher's desk
hung a bigger-than-life, black and white photograph of the *Führer*.
It always hung crooked, and I wondered why nobody ever straight-
ened it out.

At home in Majkow, my parents adjusted to their new and demanding routines as managers and caretakers of a country estate
covering 540 acres. Despite initial difficulties, my mother located
the elderly Polish owners who had been relocated to an apartment
in Warsaw. They had been moved so fast that they had to leave
most everything behind. My mother arranged to pack and ship to
them all of their table silver and some personal items like photographs. Now I wonder if they ever got their belongings, or if they
disappeared somewhere on the way. For my mother, occupying

somebody's house was just barely acceptable, given our own circumstances. Keeping their valuables definitely was not.

Our new routines slowly came to somewhat resemble the lives that Grandmama and my father had enjoyed in Avanduse before the 1917 revolution, only on a much smaller scale. We had no cars, only horses. Ulf and I went to school by carriage or, when the weather was good, by bicycle. Other trips to Kalisz and the railroad station involved the coachman and the carriage horses. Bibi and Lola were my mother and father's saddle horses, respectively, and they were also our favorites between the traces. My mother planned all of the meals together with Maria, the Polish cook, and supervised the canning of fruits and vegetables in the summer and the butchering of pigs in the fall. She trained Lisa and Bronja, the two young Polish chambermaids who had greeted us on arrival, how to serve at table.

My father was mostly invisible except at *Mittagessen,* the midday meal. He spent his time planning and overseeing the work in the garden and fields, dairy barn and grain storage. Majkow had a herd of 100 dairy cows, thirty-six work horses and four carriage- and saddle horses. As a go-between with the farm laborers, my father retained the established manager, Mr. Kerinski. I avoided him whenever I could. Mr. Kerinski spoke in clipped, bad German and referred to his own people as *faule Polacken* (lazy Polacks). Already in the morning he smelled of alcohol. When inspecting the work in the fields, he was never without a whip, the kind commonly used by huntsmen to control their hounds. Maria told me that he not only beat the peasants but also his young wife. It was hard for me to understand why my gentle father employed such a brutal man. I never dared ask.

Father converted the farm to large scale vegetable gardening as soon as the existing traditional crops ripened. Out went most of the sugar beets, potatoes and wheat. In their place, he put half of the fields to tomatoes, cucumbers, red and white cabbage and green beans. He enlarged the orchards by adding sweet cherry trees. When he found a profitable market for fresh flowers, he commercially grew gladiolas. The Tomato Baron's expertise in greenhouse growing of high value tomatoes translated overnight into success outdoors at Majkow.

At the same time he reaped his first profits in truck gardening, Grandmama began complaining that her eyesight was deteriorating rapidly. She even had trouble doing her favorite two-deck solitaire, a game she called Patience. Grandmama needed somebody to read to her and help with her huge correspondence with friends and relatives all over the world. My parents found a personal secretary and companion for her. Fräulein Lukas arrived at the same time as Grandmama acquired Putzi, a new terrier puppy.

The puppy slept on silk pillows in Grandmama's room and ate table scraps from a silver bowl. Fräulein Lukas slept next door to Grandmama and took all her meals with us. With unquestionable loyalty, she devoted herself to any of Grandmama's many whims and wishes. I never heard Fräulein Lukas complain about the midnight wall knocks coming from next door, requesting a re-adjustment of the Swiss chard leaves on her head.

Every morning, right after breakfast, a nervous Fräulein Lukas, wearing her thick glasses, read Grandmama's mail. I remember her monotonous voice droning on and on about long-winded family events and uninteresting gossip. Sometimes she had to read a long letter twice, because, when she came to the end, Grandmama had forgotten what had been said earlier. Afterwards, if there was still time, Fräulein Lucas read the German-language newspaper. By then her head would tremble so severely that she had to stop periodically to gather her composure and quiet her head. I was told that it was a nervous condition.

My mother never complained about Grandmama. But when the tension between them became unbearable, she disappeared with a migraine. My parents' bedroom was then off-limits to anybody except my father, me and Achti. The Irish setter lay next to her on the floor just as motionless as my mother in her bed. Her eyes were closed and her forehead was wrapped with a silk scarf. The room was dark, the curtains tightly drawn. She hardly ever spoke, only to ask for a new cold compress for her head. Days later, she emerged seemingly refreshed and filled with new energies to face the multitude of family and household tasks.

Ulf and I had trouble with Grandmama too. It was obvious to Ulf and me that how we had turned out was not what she had hoped for. So we tried to stay out of her way, yet at the same time we equally enjoyed getting on her nerves.

Grandmama particularly disliked the fact that my friends and I hung out with the farm hands. The manager of the dairy barn, to my delight, tolerated my attempts to teach my school pals how to milk a cow. When this became boring, I suggested we watch "how the cows do it." But this very special privilege came at a price. I told them that they would have to hand over some of their pocket money. When they eagerly agreed, I took them to a louvered window in an upstairs hayloft, from where we could see everything in the breeding pen but remain invisible to anybody else. My friends thought cattle breeding far more sensational than sucking on cheap lollipops in town.

Grandmama equally did not approve of my friendship with the one-eyed Polish blacksmith. He had lost his eye from a flying piece of hot coal when working the bellows. I loved to hold horses for him. All of our horses had to be hot-shoed, a process that made many quite nervous. Helping calm the animals made me feel useful, proud to be allowed to do a job otherwise reserved for a man. There was one small thing in our relationship that troubled me. Every time I stopped by to help, he waved a blackened plaster bust of a man in front of my face.

"My hero, Jozef Pilsudski," he said. "A great revolutionary. It's because of him that we were freed from the czar. I wish he were still alive—to free us one more time."

I was not sure what he was saying, but from his tone I thought I'd better not ask.

Not surprisingly, my barnyard distractions had a disastrous effect on my school work. At the end of fourth grade, our school director told my mother that, unless I was tutored during the summer, I would have to repeat the grade. That's how another person came to live with us. For two hours every day Drena Langei, my father's first tutor in Avanduse, tutored me in German, Latin and math. Piano lessons were later added.

Now white-haired, Frau Langei was a strict but kind teacher. Memorizing Latin vocabulary from her was a lot more fun than from my Latin teacher in school. I equally remember her for her innovative ways in helping me with the multiplication tables. I was allowed to call her by her first name, but Drena had to come back again in the summers of 1942 and 1943.

Hitler declared war on the Soviet Union on the first day of summer, June 21, in 1941. I was so wrapped up in my farm vacation that I only remember the day as being unusually hot. Nothing else about it mattered. The linden trees were blooming in the park and the air was filled with their sweet aroma. Honey bees were buzzing everywhere. My thoughts were on my parents' promise of a pony if I did well with Drena.

One day in July, my father returned from the Kalisz horse market with several field horses and two ponies. "The gray one is for you and the little bay mare is for Ulf," he said. "The horse dealer was sure that the ponies had been war booty from Russia. When he saw my interest in the gray, he said that for a slightly higher price, he would sell me the two."

My pony was fat, shaggy and had a mind of his own. I called him Max. Even today, when I close my eyes, I can feel the moist velvet muzzle touching my cheeks. I can still hear his nicker when I came with treats. Nobody else in my class had a pony, and certainly not a dappled-gray. I loved him more than anybody else, more than my father, more than my mother.

Ulf called his pony mare Trixi. We only rode bareback. Father

My brother, Ulf, my mother and me, 1943.

gave us brief instructions and then turned us loose. "You first have to learn to ride without a saddle," he said. "Shift your weight when you want to make a turn. Hang on with your legs and leave the reins alone."

The ponies grew naturally into going as a pair. Ulf thought that by the end of the summer we had gotten so good that we should try to stand on their backs like we had seen in a circus.

At first, I couldn't stand up longer than a split second before coming off. Then I discovered that falling off and landing on my feet was also a real sport. Trixi and Maxi enjoyed our games just as much as we. They stopped and waited for us to remount. We got so good at riding as a pair that we were sure any circus would love to have us.

That summer was probably the last one that Ulf and I played together. Being three years older, he was demanding a BB gun for Christmas ("Too many pigeons around here."). He went off to prep school in the fall. My mother then made the time available to ride out with me occasionally. I loved these rare moments to be alone with her. She once confessed that when she was my age, she dreamed she was married to Frederick the Great, the Prussian King. "I thought it would be most enchanting to live with him as his queen in the fairytale Sans Souci castle in Potsdam," she said. "I dreamed of us strolling together down his bewitching terraced garden."

In August of 1942, we celebrated Grandmama's 80th birthday. Fräulein Lukas and Drena collaborated on the script—in rhyme—for the skits. Luckily, this time we did not have to run on all fours pretending to be dogs, as we did for Grandmama's 75th. Our costumes represented Grandmama's interests. Ulf wore his Hitler Youth uniform (he had just recently joined) to evoke Grandmama's interest in Hitler and his war. Gertrud, a visiting younger cousin, was dressed in traditional Sicilian costume, recalling the many happy winters Grandmama had spent in Palermo and Syracuse. My part was to represent flowers and to talk like a rose. I was dressed in a white organza dress with a wide pink sash around my plump waist, and in my curled hair, I endured a prickly crown of red roses fresh from the garden. I don't remember anything else about the day, except poor Gertrud's teary complaint at the end of dinner. Being the

Grandmama's 80th birthday: cousin Gertrud, Ulf and me.

youngest one there, she was always last to be served at the table. "When Bronja came to me with the dessert tray," she sobbed, "the cake was all gone. It was just an empty plate with a few crumbs."

The initial successes of German troops in the Soviet Union raised Grandmama's enthusiasm for Hitler's war. She rallied with each daily radio report of a victory. Grandmama had hated Bolsheviks her entire life. At eighty years old, she felt herself too old to join the NS Party, but she supported Nazism in its anti-communism propaganda. She hoped that Hitler would conquer the Soviet Union and return the Baltic Germans to their pre-World War I status in Latvia and Estonia. I remember her regularly exulting that our present lives were just temporary and that soon we would return to Avanduse.

I also remember my father avoiding any reference to Hitler and the war in my presence and the strained silences with which he greeted his mother's Nazism. Even I could tell that her pro-Nazi feelings drove another wedge into her relationship with my father. One time it erupted openly. Grandmama, against all the rules of our dinner table etiquette, started to talk about the German military victories at the eastern front. Up till now, dinner conversations had mostly evolved around the weather and agricultural subjects or family and friends. We children were allowed to talk only in answer to adult questions. Not that I cared; I was grateful to be spared.

"Let me tell you about the military news I heard on the radio," Grandmama began one noontime, right after we had settled in our chairs. "Hitler's army was again successful, despite Soviet resistance. We've seized two strategic points west and south of St. Petersburg. And what a pity you couldn't hear Hitler's speech. He's just what we need—a strong leader. He'll do great things…we're going back to Estonia."

It was as if a bomb had hit the room. My father pushed his chair back and threw down his napkin.

"Mamá, I will not have politics discussed here." He then stormed out of the room.

I was stunned. I had not heard my father talk or act like this ever before. I stole a look at Grandmama for her reaction. She sat straight and serene at her place of honor, to the right of my mother, who with downcast eyes tugged nervously at her napkin. Fräulein Lukas' face was flushed and her head trembled. Ulf had a smirk on his face. After dinner he asked me if I could keep a secret.

"Now this you really cannot tell to anybody," he whispered. "Promise?" I promised. "Sometime soon," Ulf continued, "I'm going to wake you up in the night and we'll turn on Oma's radio. I'll try to find a station that is forbidden. The SS will kill us if they find out."

Suddenly I remembered the slogan *"Feind Hört Mit"* (The Enemy Listens Too) painted on storefronts in the city. I was sure that the slogan was there just for me. "I'm not sure I want to do this," I said.

"But you promised, remember," were his last words.

It wasn't until sometime during Christmas vacation that Ulf woke me up. "We're going to listen now," he whispered. We tip-toed in our pajamas to Grandmama's radio sitting on a credenza in the living room. "Close all the doors, quietly," Ulf said. "Now I will find the BBC."

What was the BBC? We hovered close to the radio and I watched as he slowly moved the needle from station to station. I was not sure what he was looking for, when suddenly he came to a place with a lot of interference.

"I think this is it," he whispered.

I listened hard but could not understand what was being said. Suddenly the voice, in German, became clear, without interference.

"The turning point has come…Germany is losing the war …Operation Barbarossa is failing…Hitler and Nazism are evil…" The radio voice broke up. I told Ulf that I was scared and wanted to go back to bed.

"Oh, you're such a sissy," he said. "But remember, you must never, ever tell anybody about what we heard. If you do, you will be killed." Then he let me go.

For Christmas, Ulf got his BB gun and I got a small lacquered mahogany carriage. The two-seater had a black-painted, waxed canvas top. It folded up or down on a hinged metal frame.

"An antique cabriolet from Italy," my father said. "What luck to find this beauty."

Having a pony with carriage brought me the same thrill that an American teenager must feel when getting a first car. Freedom to come and go as I pleased!

By the spring of 1943, my life in Majkow was only lightly supervised. I had made myself more or less independent of the rest of the family. On my own, I decided to join the Jungmädel, the Hitler Youth organization for ten-to-fourteen-year-old girls. The *Jungmädel* were formed to have *Spiel, Sport und Spass* (Play, Sport and Fun), as the slogan went. I joined because I had my heart set on winning a *Siegernagel* (Victory Pin) in the track events that the group sponsored, and you had to be a member to run. The National Socialist Party had a different category for older girls, the BDM. These initials stood for *Bund Deutscher Mädchen* (German Girls Association), but my cousin Karin joked that it really meant *Bubi, drück mich* (Buddy, Squeeze Me).

I was big on sports at school. In the winter and during bad weather, we practiced gymnastics and played *Völkerball* (a version of dodge ball—if an opponent hit you with a thrown ball, you were eliminated). In the spring came track. Much to my parents' surprise, I was fast at the dashes. Winning wasn't enough. The *Jungmädel Siegernagel* went only to runners who broke the school record. I did this in the 60-meter dash. It didn't bother me that Oberst Mölders Schule had only existed for two years. My parents came to the ceremony. I wore my *Jungmädel* uniform, a white short-sleeved shirt and a black skirt. The stadium was draped with Nazi banners: *Deutschland Siegt!* (Germany Wins!) shouted from a dozen places. A loudspeaker announced my name. I stepped up to the temporary platform and felt really proud when our principal and track coach shook my hand and pinned on my badge, the German eagle inside a wreath of leaves of oak.

Because of my youth, and my parents' distinct lack of interest in politics, this was my most intense contact, ever, with the Nazis.

I cannot remember exactly when Fräulein von Voigt came to live with us. But she arrived sometime in 1943. She had grown up in Riga, Latvia, and came to work as father's estate secretary and bookkeeper. Her classic good looks made everybody take notice. Especially, I slowly realized, my father. Helene von Voigt was self-confident, in control of anything she was doing. Clothes looked great on her tall, slender figure. In the first years at Majkow, her competence was such that my mother relied on her to run the house-hold when she suffered her migraines. On special occasions, like the autumn hunting party, the brunette beauty outshone everyone in a green gossamer silk dress covered with large white polka dots.

I have good but also painful memories of one of those parties. In the early morning hours the invited hunting guests arrived in carriages, looking for pheasants and hare to shoot. The local gun dealer was invited to this event along with friends and neighbors. Like all other munitions, shotgun cartridges were strictly rationed. By inviting the dealer, my father hoped for an extra supply.

For weeks in advance, my mother and Fräulein von Voigt planned the menu for the evening party following the hunt. My family, I later learned, was notorious for the ordinariness of its table. For this hunt, my mother thought she had a brilliant idea. She instructed Maria to make cocktail sausages out of mink carcasses that were supplied by the flamboyant Baroness Bella von Ungern Sternberg. She and her husband, originally also from Estonia, were my parents' good friends, neighbors and the owners of a mink ranch.

"Bella said that mink meat tastes better than pork anyway and I would get the meat for free," my mother said later. "But, Bella added that I should keep the recipe a secret and not tell any of our guests."

A sumptuous spread of party food surrounded the central Meissen tureen filled with the homemade meatballs in a tomato sauce. The party guests, chilled from being outside all day, devoured the food, together with much Russian vodka and Hungarian wines. The gun dealer fell out of tune. Incapacitated by vodka, he lolled in his chair, babbling about his bad luck and all the pheasants getting away.

Suddenly, a guest somehow learned of the mink lurking in the meatballs. Did he or she relish the taste and ask a maid for the recipe? The news spread like wildfire from one guest to the next. The reaction was swift. Rodent flesh! With amazing speed, the guests fled the party. Food and drink were abandoned on the table. Only the unconscious gun dealer remained. This opened an unexpected opportunity. While my parents said good-bye to their fleeing guests in the hallway, Ulf and I drank everything in sight. We even managed to fill up for more before Lisa and Bronja could clear the sideboard.

Not surprisingly, we spent most of the night bent over toilets. The next day was spent with the most horrendous hangovers locked up in solitary confinement in our separate rooms. The gun dealer fared better. Since he was unable to walk on his own, my father asked our coachman to hitch up a team and take him back into town.

To understand how my parents so easily adopted to the new life in Majkow, on the surface at least, one must appreciate my father's unusual childhood and upbringing as the only heir to an exceptionally large estate in Estonia.

Chapter 5

My father was born on January 13, 1897, the second son to my grandparents, then living at Avanduse. They named the baby Karl Ernst William and almost from the start called him Bill. He was turned over to a wet nurse, just as his brother Tuve had been eleven years earlier.

His first great shock came at the age of five, when Tuve died of tuberculosis. Four weeks before, the sensitive teenager had written his last poem. Father kept it among his most sacred possessions. It was dated April 2, 1902.

Flight of Thoughts

Silent lies forest and field
And the green glen.
I want to fly through the world
To take it all in.
The sun stands at the gate
And will go under.
From its rays sunder
Sweet tender waves.
They waft soft around me
And kiss my soul.
Life, don't leave me in the dust! Death, I flee thee!
But if tonight's the last night
For all here that I am given,

I have despite all been blessed,
Wrapped in this sun's caress.

My father, who worshiped Tuve, remembered the funeral. His parents chartered a special train to bring the coffin and funeral party from the sanatorium in Tallinn to Rakke, the station closest to Avanduse. A fleet of eighteen carriages, drawn by black horses, were waiting in a pouring rain for the coffin and mourners to arrive and be taken to the Simuna cemetery. My grandparents were known to keep exceptional horses and had at least fifty. But even they lacked thirty-six blacks to pull the assortment of coaches, coupes, cabriolets and gigs. Grandmama had ordered a dye job on the chestnuts and bays. Colorfast dyes had not yet been invented. Under the amazed eyes of rain-soaked relatives and guests, most of the horses reverted to the colors that God had intended. The almost impassable brown muddy road beneath them now ran with rivulets of black.

Tuve was buried next to the same 17th-century wooden church where, sixteen years earlier, he had loudly demonstrated a healthy set of lungs by crying through his baptism.

Common wisdom says time heals and life goes on. But for Grandmama, life came to a stop. An excruciating sadness, a great depression settled in her heart. She took to reading the Bible every day. She wrestled with her doctor's prognosis that another full-term pregnancy was out of the question. She had suffered a dozen miscarriages to produce her two sons. The risk of suffering others fought with the pain of losing her firstborn. She spent hours lying awake at night agonizing. To help with her sleeplessness, she took the advice of a friend.

"Just do what I say," Anna von Ungern said. "Have Mr. Sörmus (the gardener) grow Swiss chard in the greenhouse. Before you go to bed, tie a few of the leaves with a scarf around your head. You'll see, sleep will come."

The remedy seemed to work. Years later, I saw her wearing this bizarre bedtime headdress still. As the months unfolded, Grand-

mama gradually decided to adopt a child as a companion for my
father. Swedish friends, the von Franckens, had fallen on hard times.
Grandmama proposed co-educating their oldest son with my
father. The boys had liked each other when the von Franckens had
visited. Sten arrived under a gentleman's agreement. He would be
encouraged to stay in close touch with his family but would be
treated as Grandmama's son.

From my father's journal:

> Drena Langei was my first tutor. Both Sten and I con-
> sidered ourselves extremely lucky to have her. We adored her
> and were thrilled when allowed, on her suggestion, to ad-
> dress her with just Drena.

> Right after breakfast we went for half an hour's walk. It
> didn't matter if it stormed or snowed, we always took that
> walk… Drena was one of the first persons to introduce us
> to the world of plants and wild animals. She loved nature
> and everything that ran, crawled and wiggled. She was much
> opposed to hunting, but because Mamá was such a passion-
> ate hunter, she kept that opinion mostly to herself.

> Much more problematic was our relationship with our
> mademoiselles (the young French tutors). Let's be honest,
> what on earth would prompt a young French woman to leave
> Paris and come to Russia? Yes, they thought that we lived in
> Russia, where man-eating bears lurked in the parks and
> wolves ran around like dogs. It was quite clear that the only
> reason to accept a tutor's position was the chance to find a
> rich husband… a rich count or Russian general. Strangely
> enough, they weren't altogether mistaken. I have heard quite
> a few Cinderella stories.

My father and Sten would put up with a long list of man-hunt-
ing mademoiselles. The alternative was unacceptable to Grandmama. Under the czar's Russification laws, all schools, even private
ones, conducted instruction solely in Russian. Said Father, "Mamá

hated everything Russian. So Sten and I were home-schooled until we were sixteen."

This steeped the boys in the family's culture. My father wrote:

> On winter evenings, the whole family, including tutors, gathered in the big hall to listen to Mamá read aloud. She was a good reader, captivating us and the adults with her dramatic presentation of a story. While she read, Papá played Solitaire. Drena, who was still with us, never looked up from her embroidery. It was never boring. The books I remember best were Gustav Schwab's interpretation of the Greek mythologies, and the novels of Walter Scott and Gustav Freitag.
>
> On special occasions, mostly Saturday nights, we were allowed to play Roulette. Papá had brought an entire roulette table back from Monte Carlo. He went there every winter to relax. When we played at home, he was always the banker. We started out with an equal capital in chips. Whoever lost their capital was allowed to take a loan. It made the game exciting. It was absolutely de rigueur to claim bankruptcy.
>
> Much later, I learned from a cranky aunt that she thought this the worst way in the world to teach children about economics. But I'm sure that, because we learned to gamble early and acquired a sense for handling money (play money that is), Sten and I were never bitten by the gambling bug...

My father found delight and instruction everywhere on the estate. Constantin, his father, had hired Josef Baron Singer-Wyssogorski, former chief forester and *Jagtmeister* (master of hunt and hounds) to Prince Nikolai Nikolaevich, the brother of Czar Nicholas II. Constantin personally disliked hunting and excursions to the woods. So the baron became my father's model:

> I loved Baron Singer as a boy. To be allowed to follow him on horseback through the woods was always magical. He knew everything. He taught me how to read animal tracks. Together we listened to the sounds of the forest, the calls of

the geese and the love-calls of the capercailzie. But his best supporter was Mamá. They shared a passion for riding and hunting. To sustain the deer population, she and Baron Singer would feed them in the winter and ruthlessly kill the wild dogs and wolves roaming the forest. They were successful in stocking the woods with Manchurian pheasants.

My father with Luna.

All this was to heighten the thrill of the hunt. Only years later, when I was an adult, did I hear rumors that there had been more to their relationship than just the obsession for hunting and riding.

My father (foreground) in Avanduse with, l. to r., two of his aunts, Gita and Stella, Mademoiselle, and tutor N.V. von Sivers.

Whatever the truth, the possibility of an affair did not bother my father. His entry on Singer and Grandmama's hunts ends by affirming his mother's feelings for his father. "I know that despite their different interests, Mamá and Papá were much in love."

Mr. Sõrmus, the talented head gardener, was given nearly unlimited funds to please Grandmama. He managed to meet her insatiable appetite for everything from oleander to roses to lemon trees. Every day there had to be something fresh and fragrant to surprise her. Heated greenhouses, rare then in the far north, became the order of the day. My father as a young boy worked along with Mr. Sõrmus and fell in love with his green thumb. "He was intelligent, passionate about gardening," he recalled. "It was his passion for plants that I have to thank for my life-long interest in horticulture."

The excitement of Christmas crowned the luxury and joy of life at Avanduse. As Father described it:

> The celebrations went on for three days. Christmas Eve and Christmas Day was just for the family. The other days were for the household staff and then for the peasants holding more skilled positions in the barnyard and garden. We had two giant trees, each decorated differently. Mamá thought that the commoners would like a gaudy tree. We helped her decorate it with brightly colored paper chains, glass balls, silver tinsel, angels with silken wings, apples and gingerbread cookies and about 70 candles. Actually, that tree was very pretty and exuberant.
>
> On the third day of Christmas, at ten minutes to three, our butler announced that the commoners had arrived. They came dressed in dark brown home-spun woolen clothes. The older women still wore their traditional caps with colorful ribbons tumbling down their shoulders. Little girls hid behind their mothers' voluminous skirts, boys stood sucking

their thumbs. But chaos erupted when Santa Claus knocked at the door. Within minutes, the dining room turned into bedlam. Trumpets were blowing, drums were drumming, toy horses were galloping and wooden trains were tooting. I was not allowed to play with these children. But Sten and I were allowed to sit with them to witness what Papá announced as the biggest show on earth.

From the attic, Papá brought down a big box holding everything needed to put on the laterna-magica show. Neither I nor the village children had ever seen a slide show, let alone a Kino (movie) as they were later called. I can still see a sequence of pictures showing Red Riding Hood and Snow White projected in color on a white wall... Scary scenes from the Rat Catcher of Hamlen were too much for the little kids. Their earthshaking screams were heard throughout the house...

Right after Christmas, my parents went south for their separate vacations. Drena took over the daily reading. Papá loved the gambling scenes of the Côte d'Azur. When in Monte Carlo he stayed mostly at the Hotel de Paris, the center of it all. Dressed in a white three-piece suit, he spent his time at the roulette table, sipping Veuve Clicquot. Mamá, on the other hand, shunned the limelight of the casinos and the champagne. She preferred to immerse herself in the world of her international artist friends living in Palermo, Florence and the Isle of Capri...

In the spring, coinciding with the return of the wild geese, my parents migrated home. With them arrived boxes and crates filled with Mamá's art treasures. She explained the history of each piece. A painting that impressed me much at the time was a Sally von Kügelgen copy of Titian's *Himmlische Liebe* (Heavenly Love). (The original, now in the National Gallery of Scotland, depicts a shepherd and shepherdess in loving embrace under the trees.) As a young adult, I thought this painting gave full meaning to the spirit of the Renaissance and the glorification of the female body. Somewhat later, a chambermaid told me that it was about something else... The maid called the shepherdess "*ebbemata naaistarahwas*" (shameless hussy).

In 1912, when my father reached the age of sixteen, his and Sten's home-education came to an end. Both boys were enrolled at Kaserahu, an aristocrat's boarding school in the provincial town of Võnnu. They did, after all, need full command of Russian to enter the university.

Their social activities took them to Tallinn, to the *Estnisches Ritterhaus* (Estonian House of Nobles), a 19th century mansion that shared the heights of the old town in Tallinn with the Cathedral. The *Rittershaft* (Estonian Nobles Corporation), founded in 1249 as the Christian invaders were consolidating their grip on Estonia, formulated government policy here. But eligible young lords and ladies also partied here at formal balls and receptions.

In the summer, the boys enjoyed a carefree existence riding horses, swimming and boating in Solitude, then Grandmama's summer residence on the Baltic Sea. Getting there required an expedition. Carriages, horses, grooms, cooks, chambermaids and mounds of baggage were shipped by train to an overnight stop at the family's spacious townhouse in Tallinn. The next day, the caravan, drawn now by the horses, proceeded the last 24 miles to Solitude. The family and servants were scattered between the main villa, the tenant farmer's house and two other cottages. A delightful summer ensued, for my family if not the hardworking help. Vladimir Nabokov, the great novelist, grew up at the same time as my father on an estate just 100 miles to the east of Avanduse. In his memoir, *Speak, Memory*, Nabokov deftly describes the unbridgeable gap that existed between the few and the many in Czarist society on the eve of the revolution. "Fatal poverty and fatalistic wealth," he writes, "got fantastically interwoven in that strange first decade of our century."

World War I was the beginning of the end for Father's academy, Kaserahu. The school building was converted into a field hospital. Some students left to join the Czarist army. Some went home. Sten went back to Sweden. My father was among the few who stayed to attend classes in empty store fronts, churches and wherever else space could be found in town. A year later Kaserahu closed completely, and my father moved back to Tallinn to finish his senior year at the *Domschule* (Cathedral School). This ancient academy, founded in the 14th century, was the only other prep school in Estonia suitable for nobles. Wrote Father:

> I lived very comfortably in our townhouse on the *Breitstrasse* (Lai Street, now, in Estonian). Mamá arranged for a live-in cook and Natalia Feodorovna Schmidt, my old Russian tutor, moved in to keep me company. In the morning we left at the same time, she to teach at a Russian school, and I to my classes at the Academy. In many ways this was a very happy time for me. Mostly because, for the first time, I enjoyed real independence.

A year later, as a graduation present, my grandparents gave my father a trip to Japan. But Czarist Russia's military and political reversals in 1916 created new army call-ups, and Father's trip was postponed. University study provided an exemption from the military, so my father applied to the University of Tartu Medical School. He was not sure he wanted a career in medicine, but the curriculum matched his interest in science and biology. Avoiding the military was important for family reasons too. Grandpapa had developed sclerosis and was increasingly unable to look after the business of the estate. My father signed up for the required minimum of classes at Tartu, then spent most of his time in Avanduse, about 30 miles to the west.

My grandparents' safety soon also became an issue. The hundreds of peasant families working the estate and their rented lands were growing restless. The war had triggered political agitation against the czar everywhere, but fervor ran especially high in Estonia. The landlords were, after all, of German heritage. More than

100,000 Estonian young men had been drafted and were now at the front fighting Germany. They and their Russian comrades were losing. Activists from Tallinn and Tartu swept the country in squads of bicycles, encouraging anti-landowner protests. In Avanduse, on some days, protests virtually stopped all the work in the fields and barnyards.

At first, the agitation sometimes seemed quaint. My father recalled that one day a group of peasants appeared at the estate manor house.

> They were shouting: "Down with the nobles. Kill the pigs. Up with the proletariat." I went out to address them. They stopped yelling and whipped off their hats. I talked about the benefits, such as the local school and infirmary that we were providing for the use of the villagers. After some foot shuffling, the protestors dispersed quietly with bowed heads.

But the protests gradually became more violent. Touring revolutionaries began torching estate mansions. A few nobles were beaten, some even killed. One neighbor barely escaped death during the burning of his house. In 1917, my grandparents finally moved to their town house in Tallinn.

My father, now twenty years old, stayed and took sole charge of Avanduse. Father's unassuming charm and invariable good manners helped him manage. The family's past generosity to the community helped too. The von Bremens had done more than build the school, pay the teacher, and provide nursing services at the infirmary. They also paid the pastor's salary and maintained the church, and helped support families through illness and hard times.

But travel grew dangerous. Newspapers and the telegraph were interrupted. Rumors abounded. Tales of looting, arson, and mass farm animal slaughter swarmed in upon my father from nearby estates. Increasingly, the reports were true.

Russia was on the verge of chaos when Social Democrats

seized political power from Czar Nicholas II in February of 1917. Affairs stabilized a little. Estonia's requests for Russian army protection from communist arsonists were finally met in May. A Russian regiment arrived at Avanduse. My father arranged quarters for soldiers and officers alike. But the soldiers, recalled from the front, were in a state of near insurrection. Some actually deserted and joined the revolutionaries.

My father stationed the jittery, almost powerless staff officers in Poidifer, his other estate nearby. One whole company of officers and men were stationed at Avanduse itself. The rest of the troops were quartered in the villages.

This arrangement, tense for everyone, went fairly well for some weeks. Then, against my father's strict orders, someone on the estate leaked word to the soldiers that stocks of alcohol were hidden behind barriers in the basement of the distillery.

When World War I had broken out in 1914, Russia had declared prohibition. The Czarist government ordered all spirits at distilleries to be destroyed or converted into denatured alcohol. Denaturing was done by adding poisonous methyl alcohol, dyed pink for identification, to all stocks of potable liquor. Avanduse had complied with that order. As my father reported in his memoir:

> One evening, a group of Russian soldiers broke into the distillery. What followed was one of the most horrendous drinking orgies I have ever witnessed. The soldiers drank the normal alcohol first, even though it was tinged pink and thus poisonous. Then they finished off a small barrel that was filled with straight methyl spirits, toxic beyond belief. By dawn our front lawn was strewn with bodies. Eventually some got up, while many others never did. The dead were quietly removed at night. I was shocked, horrified and said so to survivors. They shrugged. Soldiers' dying, they indicated, wasn't important. They always did. It was God's will.

Three days later, an official inquiry was launched. Nothing came of it. A Workers and Soldiers Council had by this time asserted control of local affairs, including the military. Few if any officers had been around to blame. The Council had been more in charge than the officers. They had nobody to punish but themselves.

The Council promised me that better control would be imposed and raids on the estate would not happen again. But soon there was another. Somebody told the soldiers that there were a few wine bottles hidden in the cellar under the kitchen. That night, the cellar was broken into, the wine was found and drunk.

Father now faced the chance that the Russians would return to raid the rest of the house. He notified the Workers and Soldiers Council, pleading for protection.

The following night, in my vigil to protect the house, I had the company of two heavily armed Russian officers and two representatives of the Workers and Soldiers Council. All five of us camped out in the library. With the help of our butler, we kept the fireplace and samovar going. To keep us awake, we drank a lot of strong black tea. The conversation stayed in obligatory official Russian. But as I recall, we didn't talk much. We could hear a few brawling soldiers outside, knocking on doors and rattling windows. But there were no attempts of a serious break-in.

In the early morning hours—we were barely still awake—one of the Council reps suddenly whispered to me in accent-free German: "Don't worry. Your ordeal will be over soon. We have orders to leave Avanduse within three days."

Not speaking German themselves, the Russian officers were quickly aroused. "What did he say? What did he say?" they asked. Judging from the Council rep's cultured German, he was well educated and probably Jewish. This might create real trouble. I calmed the officers by changing the subject: "Don't worry. The sun is almost up."

The next day, a delegation of four soldiers came searching for more alcohol. My father knew his father had some vintage Bordeaux hidden behind a trap door in the attic. "I was afraid that they might find the wine and scared what they might do," writes Father. "My heart was pounding so loudly I thought they might hear it."

My father tagging along, the soldiers went carefully through the whole house. The attic was the last place they looked. Having no ladder to reach the trap door, they made a human one by standing on each other's shoulders. The top soldier unlatched the trap door, glanced into the darkness and shut it immediately with a bang. "Nothing but ghosts up there," the top soldier said gravely. "Like most Russian peasants of the time," father remarks in his memoir, "he was deeply superstitious. There was profound belief that ghosts, spirits and the supernatural haunted all strange, dark spaces."

As promised, the regiment left a day later, but my father's troubles were far from over.

Chapter 6

Early that summer, renegade soldiers, brandishing rifles, showed up at Avanduse and demanded that my father hand over the cash box. Father complied. The bandits then marched off, but immediately torched the house of a neighbor. My father on the spot decided that it was time to join his parents in Tallinn. But before leaving, he needed to hide the family silver. He chose a cavernous dead space within the foundations, one which could only be reached by prying up floorboards in a small room.

We had to work in total secrecy. Only our head coachman, Mr. Widder, and the trusted carpenter, Mihkel Leesmann, were in on the project. Stored was silver tableware and the English hunting guns. The work was done by night, and the floorboards were replaced without a trace.

Within months, life became almost as dangerous in Tallinn. Outright revolution arrived. Estonian Bolsheviks seized the *Schloss,* the parliament building, in November, just weeks after Lenin's October revolution in St. Petersburg. The Estonian Reds had the Leninists' full support. Confiscations and arbitrary arrests of both the nobility and Estonia's social democratic revolutionaries swept the land.

The family townhouse remained something of a haven until the night of January 31, 1918. Father and my grandparents woke to heavy pounding at the front door. "In the stillness of the night, it was so loud that it could have woken the dead in their graves," my father later wrote.

Four heavily armed revolutionary soldiers ordered Father to dress and follow them. They were not interested in Grandfather, who must have looked too sick for them to care. The Bolsheviks ignored Grandmama's plea that her husband was in such poor health that she needed her only son. "I assumed that it was just my time to be interrogated," Father later wrote. "I got dressed and pocketed my wallet with some money. I also foolishly took my gold watch."

He was marched at gunpoint to the *Schloss* on the *Domberg* and led to its Great Hall. It was teeming with revolutionary soldiers, interrogators and Baltic Germans—some women but mostly men. My father knew most of the prisoners belonging to the nobility. Many were distantly related to one another—the von Bremens to the von Sivers to all the von Ungern Sternbergs, and the von Pistohlkors to the Baron Wrangells to all the von Kursells. For one strange moment, my father felt weirdly reassured. He was in the best company; all the leaders of the Baltic German community were present.

Behind long tables sat Russian and Estonian revolutionaries confiscating valuables from all new arrivals. They were accused of treason to the revolutionary cause, each being charged as "an enemy of the state." As Father reports:

> While still standing in line, I was lucky enough to slip my gold signet ring and the solid-gold chain to the daughter of a friend of Papá's. She hid my valuables in her extravagant hair-do. This was topped by a big woolen hat. My valuables went out with her when she was taken back home to her mother.

When it was my father's turn, he handed the sour-looking revolutionary his wallet, cash and watch. The items were listed with my father's name and placed in a small paper bag, then tossed into a big burlap sack.

The revolutionaries took until early morning to register their prisoners and liberate their valuables. The 300 male internees, most of them Baltic Germans, were transported to the harbor and locked up on a spacious floor of an empty grain elevator.

"At this moment, my exhaustion had come to a point of no return," Father wrote. "All that I can remember is that I lay down right where I was standing, fully clothed, and slept for a very long time."

When my father woke up, the other prisoners had already formed a council under the leadership of Adam von Gernet. My father, one of the youngest men there, felt honored by appointment as von Gernet's assistant. The appointment involved passing orders to the other prisoners and requesting supplies from the outside world, especially from a newly created Committee to Help the Prisoners. This had been formed by the prisoners' female relatives, who were temporarily at least being allowed to stay in their apartments and town houses in Tallinn. "In my new position," wrote Father, "I was permitted to attend the council meetings. This made time go altogether faster and my life as a prisoner much easier."

On the third day of their internment, the prisoners received their first hot meal, a thick pea soup, prepared by the ladies of the Committee. Since the Bolsheviks were unable to provide food or bedding to the freezing cold elevator, the Committee ladies were allowed to deliver meals, mattresses and extra blankets. "The situation was extremely chaotic," my father noted. "So much so that we even had to share our meals with the guards since they were not provided for by their superiors."

Ten days later, in the middle of a cold but moonlit night, the prisoners were woken up by threats and shouts: "Pack up, we're moving out!" Again, under gunpoint, they were marched from the elevator to the gymnasium of the *Domschule,* where they were joined by more prisoners. Among them were Father's future father-in-law, Eugen von Pistohlkors, and his son Leon.

On February 20, 1918, the prisoners were taken by truck to a train station north of Tallinn, where they were loaded into cattle cars. Each car, filthy with dirt and animal waste, contained newly built double-decker platforms. Each platform held six men for sleeping. In my father's car, number 8, were twenty-six prisoners. The *tepluschka,* an iron stove resembling the potbelly, stood in the middle of the wagon, providing heat and the means for heating water. The prisoners were barely settled when a new set of revolutionary zealots arrived to be their guards.

Unfortunately for us, the new guards were from a regiment of Latvian sharp-shooters who had deserted the Czar to serve as Lenin's personal bodyguards during the October Revolution. The cars, of which there must have been fifteen to eighteen, were swiftly locked from the outside and we were off. Rumors went wild about where we were going.

Was it to the notorious gulag in Brasov or to a prison in Siberia? Opinions differed on which place was worse. Everybody exchanged horror stories, but no one had actually been to either one of them...

Soon we settled into pitiful daily routines. But we were fortunate to have two travelers among us who were not prisoners. One was Georg von Sivers, who traveled as "commissar," representing the Soldiers and Workers Council of Estonia, the Bolshevik government. Von Sivers was among those officers who had served in the Czarist army, but later deserted to support some part of the revolution. He was likely a democrat, placed on the train by Bolsheviks to assure the safety of the prisoners as the war thundered on.

The prisoners knew that the German army had launched an offensive into Estonia in early February. The Germans had been nearing Tallinn when the prisoners were abruptly shipped east. They could have been headed for simple slaughter. But my father hoped they might be pawns in a larger negotiation. As he later wrote in his memoir of the trip:

A German occupation must have been anticipated by the Soviet powers. Presumably, Lenin had given orders to keep the Baltic German nobility hostage as a stake in future war-or-peace negotiations...

The second non-prisoner on the train was a woman, Lia von Stryk. She had come along to assist the only doctor, Baron Mirbach, who was also a prisoner. They had some success; hundreds of prisoners got sick, but only a few died...

Traveling in cattle cars to Siberia was not the way any of us would have chosen, but it turned into quite an adventure. We were lucky that only two people died on the 3-week trip to Krasnoyarsk, in the middle of Siberia.

The cattle cars were locked. Our only contact with the outside world was through two ventilation shutters close to the ceilings. These shuttered windows were also used as our only open-air latrines. To reach them, we had to climb onto one of the sleeping platforms and balance ourselves in such a way that we did not fall out. It offered an unusual picture, especially when the 18-or-so-wagon train entered into a long curve...

About twice a day the train stopped at a small railroad station. The guards unlocked the heavy sliding doors and opened them just enough to shove in the meager ration. It mostly consisted of bread and tea, and a new supply of firewood. Without a round-the-clock heat from the *tepluschka*, death would have arrived swiftly in the sub-zero Russian winter. Each cattle car, in series, also dispatched one emissary to fetch fresh water.

The water collections were nerve wracking. The guards became frenzied. To scare us but also to speed up the water-fetching activity, they shot salvoes into the air. Simultaneously, each water emissary in turn was screamed at with the foulest of language. As a direct result, only one of us—and always the same person—was considered "bulletproof" enough to bring back the precious water for tea.

Some of us had managed to sew money and jewelry into the linings of coats und underwear. With this money we occasionally were able to purchase extra food. Not that it was permitted by the guards, who threatened to shoot anybody if caught. Often we sat for hours and hours at small railroad stations waiting for another train to pass coming from the opposite direction. At those long layovers, our guards relaxed their watch, and with extreme caution we could negotiate for food through the small wagon windows. Peasant women were eagerly selling bread and bacon. The most desirable bread was the *bublitshki*. The ring-shaped buns hung like necklaces on the friendly peasant women. Dried, they will keep for a long time. But fried in a pan, they will turn into a soft, fragrant delicacy…

One incident during the first week left a vivid impression. Our train again had been shunted to a side track. A brightly lit luxury express train came thundering past, also heading east. It carried the Siamese diplomatic delegation, which had been stationed in St. Petersburg. We figured that the diplomats were fleeing the city, which had become unsafe even for the diplomatic corps. With envy I watched the heated and opulent club and dining cars rolling past, just meters from my cattle car.

Some days later, we stopped again to wait for the arrival of a new engine from up the track. To everyone's surprise, we were sidelined next to the diplomats' train. Something terrible had happened. The windows and doors were shattered. The Siamese silk wallpaper hung in shreds, and the elegant mahogany furnishings had been stripped and taken away. Gone were the oriental carpets. There was no sign of life. What had happened to the diplomats? Had they been killed in a raid? *Sic transit gloria mundi.*

We wondered if that could happen to diplomats, what

might happen to us? Cold nights turned into cold days. The endless hours of travel through the monotonously dark and snowy Russian countryside made us lose track of time. But there was one thing we were all certain of now. We were taking the northern route going east. We were destined to hook up with the Trans-Siberian Railroad at Chelyabinsk in the Ural Mountains. The hook-up occurred, and the countryside became utterly empty. The only sign of human habitation was the infrequent railroad stations. Food supply became even sparser. Many prisoners, including myself, became sick with the flu.

All we could do was hope not to die. I was so sick that all I wanted to do was give up and sleep. I slept for many days and nights. Most likely my ability to sleep in those awful conditions saved my life. We were cold all the time. So cold, in fact, that my fur-lined overcoat froze to the inside wall of the cattle car. It took some pulling to get it off, but permanently left a fabric patch stuck to the wall…

What made me bear these hardships was the wit and humor of my fellow prisoners. The jokes and quips about our guards (they did not speak German) worked like powerful tonic. The few complaining insufferable souls among us were quickly ignored, then ostracized.

On the other side of the Ural Mountains, the seemingly endless virgin woods vanished; the landscape became a hopelessly flat, treeless and undulating white plain. They passed through the snow-covered swamps of Ob. The stations now seemed impossibly distant from one another. The prisoners had entered the Siberian heartland. Irritation with each other, with the guards, with uncertainty over their fate mounted. General depression set in. Occasionally a prisoner even quarreled with a guard. One led to the most memorable event of the trip.

Roman von Tiesenhausen, angered by a particularly

brutal guard, violently berated him. Without losing a minute,
the guard coldly ordered von Tiesenhausen to take off his
fur coat, and nudged him at gunpoint onto an open platform of the caboose while he watched him from inside of
the standing train. This was a death sentence! The temperature was well below zero; he would freeze solid in his shirt
sleeves in a few hours once the train got underway. But as
the train began to move, von Tiesenhausen jumped off the
platform and disappeared into the darkness of the night. By
the time the emergency brake was pulled and the train
stopped, he had worked his way into the deep snow and
oblivion. The guards made no show of searching. The es-
capee was left for dead.

The prisoners sank deeper into depression. Only much later
they learned that von Tiesenhausen ran into immortal luck. Just as
his strength was giving out, jogging coatless through the deep
snow, he saw a light in the distance. Somehow he made it to what
turned out to be a hut. He woke the peasant within and blurted out
his story, assuming the man to be a royalist this far into Siberia's
wasteland. The peasant broke into a big smile and assured the fugi-
tive that he had come to a good place. For the right kind of money,
he could arrange for a new passport, giving him a Russian name.
Thanks to the money von Tiesenhausen had sewn into his long underwear, he was ready to buy. He stayed with the Czarist farmer for
a few more weeks, mainly to assure himself that any search for him
had been called off.

With his new passport and a new coat, he boarded a passen-
ger train going west to St. Petersburg on the Trans-Siberian Railroad and reached home before any of his fellow prisoners. They
had counted him as the third person who had died on the train.

One day, a rumor spread that we were about to arrive at
our final destination. We had no idea where that would be,
but within minutes the train stopped. For the first time in

three weeks, all the cars' doors were unlocked at the same time. The guards issued orders for us to collect our few belongings. We were formed into ranks and marched off to what I now realized was the notorious prison of Krasnojarsk.

The huge seven-storied prison towered over the rest of the low wooden houses in the small town. We were housed in 25 cells, all on the 6th floor. I and nineteen others were assigned to prison cell number 2. They were: Walter von Samson-Himmelstjema, Baron Otto von Taube, Konrad von zur Mühlen, Konrad von Grünewaldt, Wolf von Grünewaldt, Baron Erik von Rosen, Bobbi von Schulmann, Gustav von Sievers, Alexander von Barlöwen, Baron Ludwig von Maydell, Baron Ernst von Manteuffel, Baron Georg von Stackelberg, Hellmuth von Lilienfeld, Baron Eckbert von Stackelberg, Oscar von Löwis, Baron Sten von Stackelberg, Wilhelm von Wrangel, Leonard von Krusenstein, Baron Tedi von Meyendorff.

Above us, on the last floor, were mostly rebellious Cossacks. And below lived all the serious criminals. Each cell was shared by 20 to 22 men, one wooden table and two large wooden buckets, called *paraschas* in Russian. Used as latrines, they were emptied once a day by a chosen honey wagon delegate. We had few contacts with other prisoners, except at meal and exercise time. From each cell one man was delegated to go to the kitchen in the basement and bring back their one daily meal. The freshly baked bread wasn't bad, it was moist and filling, but the soups were watery and thin and gave us indigestion. But the food was a great deal better than what we heard prisoners were getting at other prisons.

Worst of all was that the prisoners had not enough exercise. Everybody looked forward to the once-a-day, 30-minute, snail-pace walk. Political and criminal prisoners walked together. Long, snaking lines wound through limited space in the courtyard. Hundreds marched, but my father concentrated on making contact with the man in front or the man behind. He was fascinated with learning their stories on why they were there. Most stories originated in jealousy, alcoholism or both, but all had led to murder.

There is an unusual code among all Siberian prisoners. Everybody discussed their particular crime openly. Secrets or holding back was not appreciated. It led to mistrust in other prisoners. That's how I learned much about death and destruction, all while breathing the most wonderful air in the world.

My father became convinced that the dry Siberian winter air not only cured all pulmonary ailments but was even better than the legendary mountain air in places like Davos, Switzerland. Everyone's tuberculosis-like symptoms miraculously disappeared over a couple of weeks, including his own. The health-giving air of Krasnojarsk led him to name this chapter of his memoirs, with obvious irony, *Meine Badereise nach Sibirien* (My Trip to the Siberian Spa). Other features of the prison were more grim, as Father writes:

> Water in the bathroom/sauna was heated each Saturday for us on a number of specified floors. For me, this turned out to be a mixed blessing. Coupled with the bathing privilege came the torture of delousing. Washing my hair with kerosene was the standard remedy. Unfortunately, the treatment never lasted and had to be repeated every two weeks…
>
> The forced intimacies of prison provided me with insights into men under extreme pressure. One of the inmates in my cell had lost his mind on the train trip here. It was of great interest to me to observe the reaction of the others. Much to my surprise, the behavior of some arrogant inmates was much gentler and kinder towards him than I had expected. It also worked the other way round. What I had previously thought of as well adjusted and charming personalities turned out to be intolerant and outright nasty.

Rumors promising the release of the political prisoners circulated constantly during the exercise walk. Most proved untrue, except the final one that arrived in mid-March. Kaiser Wilhelm II, so the story went, had personally intervened with Lenin on behalf of the 500 or so Baltic German prisoners in Krasnojarsk at the peace treaty negotiations at Brest-Litowsk. The treaty had been signed on March 3. As Father reports, this turned out to be true: "Overnight the doors on the 6th floor were unlocked and we were told that we were free to go."

Go, but where and how? The wardens simply released them into the street several thousand miles from home. They milled about discussing their next move. Then, miraculously, Georg von Sivers reappeared. While the prisoners were locked up in prison, he had lodged outside the prison walls. Sivers had been able to communicate with the outside world and announced that he had just obtained enough funds from the Swedish Consulate in Krasnojarsk to finance the prisoners' journey back. Writes Father:

> Adam von Gernet was renamed Interior Minister, and I again became his assistant. Brümmer was chosen Foreign Minister and Dehn became the all important Supply Officer. With the Swedish money, Dehn purchased bread, beans, butter and meat. Whole frozen heifers were bought and loaded onto the newly organized train. But we still had a problem. We needed armed guards to escort us through a politically torn and chaotic Russia. Specifically, we needed protection against looters and from local Bolshevik attacks. Armed groups, all claiming to be Soviets, roamed everywhere.

The ex-prisoners received another stroke of pure luck. The Latvian guards who had brought them to Krasnojarsk had been stranded. In the tumult of revolution, they'd been left penniless, without orders or regular rations, or any claim on transportation home. And they still had excellent revolutionary credentials. The tables were ripe to be turned.

These young Latvians, some younger than I, were very homesick. They were desperate for transportation, money and food. They gladly accepted our offer to be our friends and guards, as long we fed and supplied them with transportation and ammunition. By now, they didn't care whom they were serving. All they wanted to do was get back home.

On the night of March 28, under the cover of darkness, so as to draw no other civilians to the rare train heading west, the former prisoners and their Latvian gunslingers boarded new cattle cars.

We were not supposed to use any light, not until we had left the station. Suddenly, just when we were getting settled for the night, a scruffy looking stowaway emerged from under one of the sleeping platforms.

His story was bizarre. He said that he was a German officer, who had been taken prisoner by the Russian Army and shipped to a military prison near Krasnojarsk from where he had escaped and taken refuge at the Swedish Consulate. When he heard that the Swedes were organizing a transport for Baltic Germans returning to Latvia and Estonia, he decided to hide in the train. Our council debated the issue and decided to let the stow away remain.

In fact, the Brest-Litowsk Treaty had stipulated that the exact number of men who had been deported had to be returned or accounted for. Two deaths had occurred on the trip to Krasnoyarsk, but somehow the disappearance of Tiesenhousen had never been recorded. So the council was officially still short one man. The stowaway came in handy—he filled the gap…

In the meantime, the ex-prisoners traveling west had no knowledge of events back home. Just one day after they had been shipped east out of Tallinn, German troops had captured the city. The Estonians were glad to be rid of the communists but were trying to set up a completely independent republic when the Germans marched in. The elated Baltic German minority, however, backed by the German army, swept them aside and set up their own carefully picked *Landesrat* (Senate), including only a few token Estonians. In early April this new government unanimously requested a union with Germany under the Kaiser. Soviet Russia, in a move to placate both the Germans and Estonians, renounced sovereignty over Estonia about the same time.

The prisoners' freedom train pulled out of Krasnojarsk under cover of darkness, the wagon doors cracked open to ventilate the box cars with fresh spring Siberian air. The prisoners' mood was ebullient, and their elite Latvian guards greased the way.

> Our guards, brandishing their weapons, supervised the changing of locomotives every couple of hundred kilometers. They also procured our fuel, mostly wood. Traffic conditions were chaotic all along the rail line. But our guards kept our waits at each stop very short. In Omsk, the local Soviets tried to stop us. The guards cleared our way by firing tremendous volleys into the air.

After that, the passage back grew increasingly difficult. As Father reports:

> The euphoria of going home quickly dwindled when we came to another crisis in Jekaterinburg in the Ural Mountains. We were sidelined next to a children's transport train from St. Peterburg. The children had been evacuated, supposedly for safe keeping, from a chaotic and starving city. The commissar in charge of the train told us their children's transport had run out of food. His own revolutionaries were armed and desperate. The commissar claimed we were counterrevolutionaries. At gunpoint he demanded that we give up some of our food. After long and hostile negotiations, "Foreign Minister" Brümmer signed a document. It stated that we were a group of Finnish princes and barons who now realized their mistake in willfully starving the children of St. Petersburg. It

also stated that we were sorry for what we had done. We were now happy to make amends by sharing our provisions with the children. Attached to this document was a list of itemized food supplies. After the transfer of bread and a frozen heifer we were allowed to proceed.

Another roadblock was thrown up in Moscow. The ex-prisoners' train was shunted by dark of night into a freight siding. Lenin's central government was being forced to hide the nobles' presence from the unruly local revolutionary Soviet government. The direct rail route to Riga via Smolensk was also closed along the line. After hours of negotiations, the central Bolshevik government ordered the train switched to tracks going southwest in the direction of Kiev. Even this detour left the Baltic nobles' position dicey. Revolutionary detachments of armed militia, police and soldiers wandered every city and town looking for Czarist sympathizers and counter revolutionaries. It was uncertain if these unruly bands would honor the central government orders in the cities along the route and let the ex-prisoners pass, even though accompanied by Lenin's own guards.

Again we were made to depart Moscow in the middle of the night. Inside the cars, we were not allowed to use any light and had to keep all doors and shutters closed. Nobody was allowed to "use the facilities" in the way I had described them earlier. We had to use buckets.

In the end, they got through. When the train reached Orsa, near the Russian provincial border, it was stopped by German troops, who still held large chunks of the Ukraine and the states along the Baltic. The Germans had no idea what to make of this group of filthy and diseased men. An exchange of many telegrams between the ex-prisoners' council and the German military occupation authorities in Riga finally cleared the way. They were permitted to disembark from their cattle cars and temporarily became guests of the German army. "We were quartered in Army tents and slept on field cots," Father wrote, "but the best thing of all was the hearty soup, the first in months, from the army's field kitchen."

My father's memoir does not describe the route from the camp back to Estonia, but when they finally reached German-occupied Tallinn at the end of April, they received a hero's welcome.

> We must have been an unusual sight, covered with lice and filth. Our clothes were stiff with dirt. They could have stood by themselves when taken off. But the reception at the train station was wonderful. A military band was playing while I was embraced by Mamá, and German General von Seckendorf personally shook all our dirty hands.

For the next two weeks, my father stayed in the family townhouse to recover from his ordeal. He got de-loused, cleaned up and, as he noted gratefully, he could once more enjoy a cigarette whenever he liked. His trip to Krasnojarsk, he told his diary, had left him with "an even deeper animus towards anything Bolshevik" than before.

It would be thirty-five years before the communists, once again, would find him an "enemy of the state." But that would be in the German Democratic Republic.

Chapter 7

In May, my father returned to Avanduse to find a bubble of calm. Revolution gripped most of the former Russian empire. But in Estonia, the German army of occupation had put the nobility back in power. The country's democratic and Bolshevik revolutionary leaders had been arrested or gone into exile. The rhythm of life, especially in rural areas, now went forward much as before. Avanduse, under my father's management, that year produced an especially good crop.

Then, on November 11, 1918, the six-month pause in tumult came to an end. Germany surrendered in the West. Overnight, German troops withdrew from Estonia. A provisional government of Estonians took power under Konstantin Päts, a Social Democrat just released from a German prison. Päts' coalition of parties was dedicated to national independence, to democracy, and to the confiscation of all lands held by the nobility. Ten days later, Soviet troops invaded Estonia to reclaim sovereignty for Russia—this time under communists.

The brand new Estonian government determined to fight. It had a trained core of Estonian soldiers who had served in the Czarist army. The British provided arms and ammunition and sent a naval force. Over the Christmas holidays, three British cruisers and nine destroyers defeated a Soviet fleet preparing an invasion of Tallinn. The beleaguered Baltic Germans now faced a quandary. With either victor, they were going to lose their estates. But the Soviet invaders were the bigger threat. In January of 1919, hundreds of Balts therefore rallied to Päts' call to arms. They formed their own unit, the *Baltenregiment* (Baltic Regiment), and joined the fight. By May, the Estonian army numbered 74,300 men, including 700 in the regiment of Baltic Germans.

My father was one of these loyalists. He joined the regiment as soon as it was formed. He loved Estonia as his homeland. A Russian-dominated Bolshevik government would leave him no chance at all to stay. The Soviets were slaughtering the nobility of Russia out of hand. My father pocketed his pistol and, in his own words:

> I saddled my horse and rode the 50 kilometers or so from Avanduse to Rakvere, where the *Baltenregiment* was being organized. I was never put under arms. A lingering problem with my lungs prevented me from being sent to the front. I was assigned a job as secretary to the commanding staff of our regiment. My duties were to process and deliver the daily orders. It was then that I learned to type on an English typewriter. I have to admit that I never got beyond using two fingers.

Unfortunately, there are no further entries in his journal. But the Estonian forces pushed back the Soviet invaders all through 1919. They defeated a final Russian Bolshevik counterattack on the border, just after the New Year, on January 3, 1920.

Lenin's regime was also battling White Russians and half a dozen invading foreign army units. Lenin now needed peace with Estonia at any price. He signed a treaty confirming Estonian independence from Russia in early February. The plucky Estonians wound up with an indemnity payment of 15 million gold rubles and about 5 percent more land than they had claimed when the war began. (Soviet Russia took back these territories when it invaded Estonia again in 1940.)

The *Baltenregiment* disbanded as soon as the peace was signed. My father rode back to Avanduse on the same horse that had carried him into the war a year before. Legislation expropriating the agricultural land and forests of Avanduse and 1,064 other Baltic German estates had been enacted by the Estonian parliament months earlier, in October of 1919. So legally, the land of the estate no longer belonged to my family. But the process of division and distribution was bound to proceed slowly. In the meantime, my father resumed management of his slowly shrinking estates. Surely, he felt, he could salvage something.

This was the first of three financial collapses that my father would surmount. He was a man of subtle strategies and persistence, smiling, dodging and outflanking fate whenever it rolled at him head on. The American cartoonist James Thurber once characterized a person exactly like my father. I remember Thurber's words to this day: "He did not yell down the demons of life and fear, instead he fought them with angels."

As my father wrote:

When I returned to Avanduse, the situation was better than I had expected. But three weeks (occupation by) Soviet soldiers had taken a toll. All the furniture was missing and the books from the library were strewn all over the empty rooms. The central heating was completely ruined. We never had it repaired again. I just couldn't get the right size pipes or the plumber to install them. From then on I lived only in the oldest part of the main house, where the beautiful ceramic tile stoves had remained and were functioning. The grizzly still stood in the hallway, but he had lost an ear. A Bolshevik must have taken a knife to it...

In the ten days following my return, I got my final surprise. Most of the furniture re-appeared. Each morning I discovered a few more new pieces sitting in a snow bank in front of the house. Eventually almost everything came back that way. No questions were asked and no answers were given. The silver under the floorboards was never discovered.

My grandparents survived the revolution in their town house on Lai Street in Tallinn. My grandfather's sclerosis had rendered him invalid. Over the early decades of the 20th century, my grandparents had donated significant lands to local Estonians whom they deemed worthy. But their holdings were still immense. The surveys, negotiations and paperwork involved in distributing individual properties to tenants stretched out until 1926. My father devised ever more intensive farming practices to keep his shrinking fortunes afloat. The stables, fish ponds, saw mill, electric generator and main distillery at Avanduse remained at first in his hands. Only producing farmland and forests had been initially confiscated. Father received token payments of long term state bonds as the land was given out. With these funds, plus a successful distillery operation and the greenhouses, the family struggled but was not destitute.

We lost Poidifer first. Just about this time Mamá and Papá decided to move to Germany. Negotiations with the Estonian land reform authorities were so unpleasant and stressful that Papá's health declined even more.

My grandparents had begun traveling in the west, seeking the best winter climate for my grandfather's health. They tried Baden-weiler in the Black Forest, Wasserburg on the Bodensee in Switzerland but finally settled in tiny Ahrenshoop on the north coast of Germany. Ahrenshoop was supposed to have the clearest air in Europe. Its simplicity and cheapness recommended itself to my grandparents' dwindling fortunes too. Said Father:

Papá's sclerosis seemed to improve here. Mamá rented *Heiderose*, a furnished villa just behind the sand dunes. She enjoyed the ambiance of the fishermen's thatched houses. Mamá became friendly with the German artists living there as well. I visited them once a year.

Despite the good air, my grandfather's condition worsened in the summer of 1924. He became confined to his bed. One of the few surviving letters from Grandmama to my father delivered the bad news:

Ahrenshoop, October 10, 1:30 in the morning
(Letter # 10)

My dear Bill, my beloved child!

Deeply saddened your mother comes to you with the news that half an hour ago your beloved father sighed for the last time. He went peacefully. I lost all hope when he refused any kind of nourishment...On October 9th, I noticed a big change in his features. He was fully conscious but also appeared in a deep sleep...When I thanked him for all the love and kindness he had surrounded me with, he smiled knowingly, as if I was lying. . . Around 10 o'clock his breathing became fainter and fainter. At midnight, he took a few deep breaths and then it was all over. . . By now you must have gotten letter # 9... I'd like to see a small announcement in the Tallinn newspaper...Please send me some money, since what I still have will not be enough to cover the extra costs... God will protect you my dear, dear child. I hug you and hold you close.

Your Mamá

My father arrived in time for the simple burial in the fishermen's cemetery of Ahrenshoop.

By the middle of 1925, Grandmama moved back to Avanduse. She and my father by then retained only the big house, the large park, one greenhouse, some of the stables and the main distillery. They also had just 32 acres left to farm. The stress produced a falling out with his head gardener. Father fired him and needed a replacement:

Through an ad in the German newspaper I found... Erika von Pistohlkors, who had just graduated from arborist school in Zwingenberg, Germany. She was now looking for a gardening position on a Baltic German estate. Her parents had already lost their seat, Immafer, and Erika was forced to look for a job… I had known about Erika and her family through her two brothers, Oscar and Leon. We had attended Birkenruh together.

Erika duly set to work in the greenhouses and orchards that still belonged to Avanduse. The close working relationship and passion for horticulture shared between them soon led to romance. Their courtship and engagement—and re-engagements—became scenes from a bitter comedy. Grandmama kept getting in the way.

In my mother's own words:

> When I entered Avanduse for the first time, I was over-whelmed by the grandeur of the house and the importance of the von Bremen family…Paps and I were engaged three times. We would get engaged when Grandmama was travel-ing. When she came back, I broke off the engagement each time…Contrary to my first impressions of her feelings, Grandmama turned against me. It took me a long time to recognize it and know that I was never, ever to be welcome.

Much later, I asked my relatives about the relationship at a family reunion. The answers struck common themes. To quote an aunt: "Given your grandmother's strong personality, she had al-ways dominated and controlled your father's life. For the first time he had made his own decision and gone against her wishes. She never forgave him. Later your grandmother transferred the dislike of your mother to you and your brother Ulf. It must have been very hard for everyone involved, especially your mother. She could never escape. Life must have been hell. But she never complained. Or did she?"

My father's financial affairs were sinking as his involvement with my mother rose. A new wave of expropriation fell on the main distillery. This was his chief source of income. Without it, the manor house, greenhouse and other properties simply could not be maintained. Worse, there was no market for large manor houses in post-revolutionary Estonia. They were simply falling to the state for back taxes. So Avanduse would be a nearly total loss.

As his wedding date neared, Father cast about for a way to stay in Estonia. He discovered that Grandmama, through a quirk in the Estonian law of nationalization, still owned Solitude, the 120-acre summer vacation property on the coast. The land, it turned out, had been registered in her name alone. The Estonian parliament, on the other hand, had nationalized only land belonging to members of the Estonian Nobles Corporation, the *Ritterschaft*. By ancient feudal tradition, membership in the *Ritterschaft* had been limited to males alone.

"By sheer accident," Father told me much later, "we discovered that Solitude had fallen between the cracks. At first we simply couldn't believe it."

Facing homelessness in 1926, father decided he could fix up the three existing houses on the property. Grandmama agreed to move to Tabu, a small wooden house in the woods. My parents would occupy the 200-year-old fisherman's roadhouse and depot in the meadow, now rented to the Estonian caretaker. This traditional one-story thatched Estonian *reheilamu* combined living quarters towards the sea with a stable in the rear. It held one cow and my father's childhood pony, Gretchen, now a 20-year-old wagon horse. The family's own spacious villa, called the *Löwengrube* (Lion's Den), was not winterized. It would be rented to summer vacationers.

My parents were married on December 16, 1926, in Rutikvere, the ancestral home of her family, the von Pistohlkors. This truly grand mansion had already been taken by the government, but my mother's parents received special permission to hold the wedding there. My father recollected in a letter:

> Most likely for the last time, the magnificent ballroom and dining room were aglitter with the lights of more than two hundred white candles. I was overwhelmed by the brilliance of light reflected in the abundant silver on tables and crystal chandeliers up above. The cold and snowy outside sparkled with the lights of the festive party inside. Long

tables, covered with damask linen, had been set up in the dining room. White-gloved waiters served from gold-rimmed white china, just like in the old days. But now that you ask, I cannot remember what we ate. As I recall, there were no flowers, just evergreen branches brought in from the park.

My parents as newlyweds at Solitude.

Your mother looked lovely in a simple white dress. It had a dropped waist line. In the late afternoon, Mamá, your mother and I left by sleigh to catch the last train back to Tallinn. We dropped Mamá off in Tallinn and continued to the resort town of Haapsalu, the destination of our honeymoon.

When they returned from Haapsalu, my mother "thought that I was about to enter a fairy tale," as she told me later. "A little stone house near the sea with my prince, a horse and a cow." The long shadow of her disapproving mother-in-law had not yet fallen on the new doorstep. The immediate problem was finding a way to earn a living. The wooded sloping property was unsuited for major conventional crops. My parents had a small income from the revenue bonds, and my father had sold off some of the equipment and furnishings of Avanduse. He had raised a small fortune selling about one mile's length of copper wire that had distributed power from the generator in the old water mill to the scattered buildings on the estate. My parents could also count on one pig, slaughtered each fall, and several sacks of wheat from the farmer who rented the 32 acres that my father still owned in Avanduse. I still remember as a child the carcass of a pig and the bags of wheat arriving early every winter on the bus. But these resources combined covered a fraction of my parents' living expenses, and their savings were rapidly running out.

In desperation, my parents and a hired girl, Elli, began cooking up batches of a caramel-like Baltic German specialty candy, *Schmantbonbons,* in the copper wash boiler of the laundry room of the vacation villa. They were less than two miles from the nearest bus stop. Packed in pretty 9-by-6 inch boxes and shipped by bus to Tallinn, their "Valencia" brand caramels became a big hit. But Solitude lacked electricity, and the bus could offer no refrigeration either. Their fresh candies lost shape in the packing and then melted on the way to market the first hot day in summer. "I was in a panic," my mother recalled. "What were we going to do now?"

But Father had been thinking about the heated greenhouses

he had built in Avanduse. His problem there had been Avanduse's great distance from any large urban market. Here, my father figured, a heated greenhouse, if it could be built, could produce tomatoes in the summer and cyclamen in the winter for the huge

Grandmama holds Ulf in front of Tabu. My other grandmother, Mary von Pistohlkors (center) and my mother look on.

market in Tallinn. The city was just one hour away by the daily bus that did double duty as a truck. To create the first heating plant, my father scavenged steam pipes from disused railway cars and found a scrapped U-boat boiler in a marine junkyard. He then served as helper to a single pipe fitter, who assembled a wood-fired greenhouse heater from the materials. My father and mother's green thumbs did the rest. By the time we fled to Poland, my parents had four large greenhouses working year round, a large summer truck garden, and had bought an apartment house rental property in Tallinn with part of their savings. They were on their way back to at least modest riches.

Chapter 8

Poland had been in the throes of mass deportation as our family arrived from Tallinn. We had heard gunfire, possibly from Nazi commandos, from our train. We had lived in one deportee's house and in Majkow, we were now living in another. Thanks to later uprisings and the death camps that exterminated more than three million of Poland's own Jews, the country was suffering more casualties in relationship to its population than any other in World War II. Despite this, secure in the incredible cocoon of my childhood, my memories of Majkow are among the happiest of my youth.

My cousins, Karin and Gertrud, came many summers for "good country air and rosy cheeks." Their parents had moved east out of Idstein, Germany, to the new Warthegau, settling in Poznan where Onkel Adolf taught architecture. Karin and Gertrud were great summer playmates, but as city girls, they were uncomfortable with farm animals and horses. This sometimes kept me away from Max, whom I was as wedded to as any Mongol. Max and I roamed the estate, riding through the park and across fields and meadows. Karin told me years later that she was scandalized by my unsupervised roaming, and that she shared Grandmama's disapproval of my familiarity in hanging out with the Polish farm workers.

But Karin had great flair of her own. She invented entertainments, one being the idea of making hats out of rhubarb leaves and selling them for pennies to anybody in the family we could corner. We three cousins and Paula, my best friend from school, would spend hours gathering the millinery materials. Then the real fun began, assembling the hats. Karin always did the best ones. She could curl and fold the rhubarb leaf just so, give it the size and shape she wanted, then secure it—as we others secured our own— with a twig or the stiff stem of a flower. Next we piled on roses, daisies, nasturtiums and zinnias. But Karin would also add anything from bird feathers and raspberry canes heavy with fruit to baby carrots with bushy tops and garlands of green pea pods. Once finished, we sat behind Grandmama's borrowed card table, cheeks flushed, waiting for customers. Grandmama and Putzi, returning from their daily walk in the park, were usually the only ones who stopped. Grandmama was always delighted trying on this hat and that before buying—always the ones made by Karin. It didn't bother the rest of us much. We wound up wearing our own hats.

Karin and Gertrud returned to Poznan at the end of summer refreshed by the country air and fresh country food, but puzzled by the smell in their rooms. "I loved the golden chairs in the great hall and I loved the grizzly with the one ear," Karin later recalled. "But I hated the blue, green and yellow guest rooms upstairs. We always had to stay in one of them and they smelled awful." That aroma stemmed from my mother's frequent burning of sulfur. No matter how hard she tried, she never totally got rid of the bed bugs in those rooms.

Winter in Majkov could hold as much excitement as summer. After a good snowfall, or even during one, I invited my school friends out. Each was required to bring her own sled and a length of rope. With cold, stiff fingers, we attached the sleds to each other, with my sled first. Then I hooked my sled to Maxi in the new harness that came with the two-seater mahogany carriage. A touch of the whip and the screaming of a bunch of girls was enough to set Maxi racing as fast as his short legs would go. Our snake of sleds tore over the wide fields. Eventually I reined the pony into a sharp turn, tipping the sleds and tumbling us all out. We swallowed a lot of snow, but that was the climax of the race and Maxi loved it too.

My best friend Paula was a fixture at our house. She came in part to escape tensions at home. Her father and mother disagreed a lot. Her father had been an early member of Hitler's SA (the party's first storm troopers) and did not approve of his family's religious activities. The Hitler Youth was supposed to be his children's sole religion. But Paula's mother insisted that all her children go to Mass often. To obey her, Paula asked me to come along on her secret trips to the only Catholic church on Adolf Hitler Platz. Since her father had his office looking out on the same square, we made mad dashes to avoid his seeing us from his upstairs windows. Once in-

Paula, Mother and me on Bibi.

side, we were totally out of breath but felt safe from his wrath. Paula taught me how to dab myself with holy water and light a candle for somebody I loved. Without telling her, I lit my candle for Maxi and prayed that we could be together forever and ever.

Paula and I remained inseparable, sharing secrets and feelings until the winter of 1945, when the *Oberst Mölders Schule* closed forever. Years later, I heard that at the end of the war, just about the time that Hitler committed suicide, Paula's father also took his life, using his Party revolver.

As an Easter present in 1942, my parents gave me a baby lamb. Lili grew into a fluffy, feisty sheep stabled in a stall next to Maxi's. During the summer, I often brought Lili into the house and Paula and I raced her up and down the stairs. Paula was aghast at seeing the fresh and pungent droppings left behind, but in our house nobody seemed to mind. There was always somebody to clean it up.

During vacations, I had to practice almost every day for my piano lessons given by Drena Langei. "And please close all the doors," Grandmama made sure to say each morning. Oh, how I hated those practices! One day I took Lili into the room with me while I labored over my assignments. Lili grew bored with the music and turned mountain goat, using the furniture for mountains. She went wild, jumping from one chair or table to another. I finally had to call a halt and take her outside. She had jumped on top of the Blüthner and struck some notes on the keyboard with her hooves. It would have been another room arrest for sure if anybody had heard or seen it.

The first cloud over my childhood idyll in Majkow was the change in mood of my parents following Stalingrad. In one of the bloodiest battles in World War II, the German Sixth Army surrendered there on February 2, 1943. Soviet battle deaths were at least 400,000, maybe higher. More than 100,000 Russian civilians were killed in Stalingrad and its suburbs. The original force of 300,000 German soldiers was reduced to 90,000 men. The victorious Red Army force-marched the prisoners to detention camps. Many died there of starvation or froze to death along the way. Only about 5,000 prisoners returned to Germany a decade later.

Bad news until then had never been reported. It might have weakened the German will. But Stalingrad was apparently too big to be ignored, and the solemn announcement of the defeat and unimaginable loss of human lives marked a turning point. My parents had never joined the NSDAP (National Socialist German Workers Party—the Nazis). I later learned that my father, as the manager of a confiscated estate in the Warthegau, had been under great pressure to join but had somehow always managed to put it off. I personally had never heard a word of praise for Hitler or the Nazis from my parents' lips. Yet my family's current good fortune in Kalisz was obviously tied to a German victory. After Stalingrad, they told me afterwards, they knew that sooner or later they would be on the move again. They kept their silence. Grandmama held on to hope. Stalingrad, she proclaimed, was just "a temporary setback."

At the time, I understood little of the details about Stalingrad, but the gravity and somber mood of my parents deeply impressed me. Something big and bad had happened. Like many German parents who were not Nazis, my parents never talked openly about events with us children. Their manner even discouraged the asking of questions. From the day we had arrived in Poland, an air of secrecy had settled everywhere, at home, in school, among my friends. One of my teachers regularly urged my class to report to her about the political thinking of our parents. The same request came from the Hitler Youth troop leader in our school. This atmosphere of suspicion seemed almost natural to me then, the way things were. But at the same time, I also knew that the suspicious silence betrayed a fear of some kind of political retribution.

Soon after Stalingrad, I noticed a change in Nazi propaganda. More banners appeared everywhere, in school and on the streets of Kalisz. A color poster showing a somber Hitler in his brown SA uniform was replaced with one showing German soldiers and civilians. The caption for it read: *Ein Kampf, ein Wille, ein Ziel: Sieg um jeden Preis!* (One Fight, One Will, One Goal: Victory at all Costs!) My favorite was the cartoon of *Kohlenklau* (coal thief). It depicted a bent-over, unshaven man in black carrying a sack over his shoulder. The poster, a symbol of stolen energy, was headlined, *Da ist er wieder! Fasst ihn!* (Here he is again! Catch him!)

In the spring of 1943, Allied forces began a fire bombing tour of cities like Berlin, Hamburg and, much later, Dresden. My parents responded to the call of a new program called *Kinderlandverschickung* (Send Children to the Country). The program provided temporary homes for bombed-out children. Four girls from Berlin came to live with us in the summer. They had not only lost their homes but also their soldier fathers. The Berliners, as we called them, were of my age. My parents hoped to provide them with a carefree summer at an otherwise grim time.

Ingeborg, Helga, Hannelore and Edeltrout, the youngest, all slept in the smelly yellow guest room. The blue and green rooms were reserved for visiting relatives and friends. To introduce the girls to the barnyard, my mother asked me to show them the litter of newborn pigs.

"We don't want to see pigs," they united in protest. "They're filthy, they stink. We don't want to touch them. They'll dirty our clothes."

I next suggested that we take a few mugs and I would show them how to milk. "There's nothing like warm milk directly from the cow," I said.

"My mother doesn't want me to drink milk that doesn't come from a glass bottle." Ingeborg was truly upset.

"Yes, and only when the bottle's been left at the door, with fresh rolls," Edeltrout chimed in.

I knew she was lying. All dairy products, as well as sugar, flour and tobacco, were rationed and home deliveries had stopped. I began to hate their living with us.

In desperation, I suggested that we check out the raspberry patch. That worked as a daily expedition for a couple of weeks.

Then I suggested the poppy field. Poppy seeds are a popular ingredient in breads and cakes in Eastern Europe. In particular, I loved the custard poppy seed torte Maria made for special occasions.

But these were special poppies. Many of the crops my father grew were obligatory for the war effort, including these poppies, which were needed for the painkiller morphine. I will never forget the magical sight of a field of opium poppies in bloom (*Papaver somniferu*). Huge saucer-shaped flowers in brilliant colors of lavender ranging to deep burgundy topped each tall stem. Some were blotched with black and came up to my chin. But by the time the girls from Berlin appeared, the poppies had long stopped flowering. The pods were now ripe, ready for harvest.

"Just break off the tops of the pods like this." I demonstrated by pouring the charcoal seeds into my mouth. Everyone agreed that this was fun and they tasted good even to the Berliners. We went back the next day and downed a whole lot more. I remember yawning, saying: "I'm so sleepy... need to lie down." I stretched out in the hot sun. The Berliners dozed off too.

When we woke up, we realized that we would be late for *Mittagessen* (noon dinner). Hurrying home from the field, we compared notes. We'd all had gorgeous dreams. They had all been filled with similar objects: shimmering round shapes in rainbow colors dancing weightlessly in a spiral. Fantastic. We pledged not tell anybody about this. And we promised we'd go again the next day.

When we arrived in the dining room, everybody was already seated, their silent eyes upon us. "Yes, and where have you been?" My mother's voice was ominous.

"We were in the poppy field and then...well, then we fell asleep," I said. I was puzzled when I saw a shocked look cross Mother's face. She glanced at the others. What had we done?

"As you can see," Mother said, "we've already started. Take your plates and eat your dinner in the kitchen!" Thank God! She seemed more worried than angry. The girls looked at each other without enthusiasm but followed me into the kitchen.

What nobody knew was that eating there was much more fun than eating at our dinner table, where we were not allowed to talk. My parent's motto: children should be seen but not heard. In the kitchen with Maria and Lisa, we could do anything. Too bad that Bronja was not with us anymore. She'd been so much fun. Months ago she was sent off to work in an ammunitions factory in Germany. At that point I did not know about the practice of slave labor. We never heard from her again.

After *Mittagessen,* my father took us girls aside. "Under no circumstance are you to go back to the poppy field," he ordered. "The poppies are grown for the war effort, not for us. Just keep that in mind."

In less than a month and much to my relief, the girls from Berlin left to live in a children's camp somewhere else. Their departure was quick and came without much explanation. One day they were still there for breakfast, the next day they were gone and the yellow room was sulfured again. I asked my mother where they had gone.

"We had an unfortunate incident," she said. "It was Lisa who told me that some silver teaspoons were missing. And then, Fräulein von Voigt noticed the small packages that Edeltrout had put in the outgoing mail basket." When Edeltrout's mother was contacted, she wrote back to say that she was sorry not to have thanked us earlier for the lovely presents. She certainly appreciated the gesture, because she had lost most everything in the bombing of Berlin. My mother sank into deep depression when she got the news that her brother Leon, a German army officer, had been killed by a sniper in September of 1943. He worked as a translator for a military staff inside the Soviet Union. Uncle Leon and his family, who were also evacuees from Estonia, had been granted an estate near us when he was summoned for the army. His loss made my mother decide to do something positive for the military. She re-activated her Red Cross nursing credentials, which she had not used since the First World War in Estonia. Dressed in a new uniform, she went twice a week to the railroad station to help with wounded German soldiers coming through. The Kalisz railroad station was a stop on a main

Mother (left) and friend on Red Cross duty at Kalisz station.

east-west line. Military trains rolled through twenty-four hours a day. They brought new troops and supplies to the front and returned with the sick, the wounded and the dead. When a train stopped, my mother and other Red Cross volunteers served hot soup from a field kitchen set up day and night. They fed the soldiers who could not feed themselves. They changed bandages and dispensed morphine to the critically injured.

While there, my mother could not help but notice other trains coming through. They were dirty cattle cars packed with Russian prisoners. The Red Cross volunteers were under orders not to talk to them or give them food. But my mother, fluent in Russian, made contact anyhow. From them she learned that they were destined for forced labor camps inside Germany. Mother was overheard talking to the prisoners. Her shocked fellow volunteers told her that by just talking to the prisoners, she could be denounced as "an enemy of the state." Severe consequences for her and her family could follow.

As time went on, I could see that her work at the station was stressful. I often went with the coachman to pick her up. In the carriage and out of public view, her face would sometimes curl into an expression of pain. She once broke down and cried uncontrollably.

"Oh, my dear child, it's all so terrible…the war…the wounded …the prisoners…the many dead…and no end in sight."

Sheltered as I had been, I actually thought that my mother was overreacting. But I kept that to myself and stopped going with the coachman to pick her up.

Brutal news from the front lines was now routinely reaching me. From Grandmama I heard about the June 6, 1944, Allied invasion of Normandy. She was the only one who talked about it. She was confident the Allies would be contained. For me France was just too far away to be overly concerned. I cannot remember if there was a discussion in school. D-day was certainly played down on German radio. It was very different with the news from the eastern front. War propaganda at the *Deutsche Wochenschau,* the weekly newsreel, intensified. In one rare visit with my mother to the movies in Kalisz, she covered my eyes with her hand.

"I don't want you to see this."

But through the gaps of her fingers I could see everything. The pictures showed Russian atrocities to German civilians in the East Prussian village of Mayakovskoye. There the Red Army had taken revenge for years of brutal German suppression in the Soviet Union. I saw piles of people who had been clubbed or shot to death. Some were crucified on the doors of their barns. When the Germans later retook the village, they filmed the scenes of horror and showed them in the *Wochenschau.* From then on I was not allowed to go to the movies.

On July 20, the failed assassination attempt against Hitler was announced.

"Thank God, nothing happened to him," said Grandmama. My mother, breaking her normal silence, questioned the quick execution of Colonel Claus von Stauffenberg and three of his fellow conspirators. She felt that these men might have had good reason for trying to kill Hitler. Von Stauffenberg and several other plotters came from old, respected German aristocratic families. My mother was concerned about possible repercussions for us and other aristocrats, even though we were related to none of those in the plot.

In August, my parents were visited by a good friend. I called him Onkel Helmut. He was a naval officer and prominent U-Boat commander on a short holiday. He was unafraid to talk, and his news was grave. He said that Hitler and his generals had lost control, that Germany was losing the war. He ignored my grandmother when she tried to argue that the war could still be won.

Later that month, something unimaginable happened. My father abruptly disappeared during the early morning hours when I was still asleep. "Paps had to go for military training," my mother explained. "We hope that he'll be back soon."

I reluctantly believed her. But his departure was so abrupt I wondered why the military training had not been mentioned before. I wondered if Paula's father or the father of one of Ulf's friends had something to do with my father's disappearance. I knew that this neighbor, also a party functionary, had pressured my father to join the party. Could two powerful men have denounced him for not keeping *Mein Kampf* in our bookshelves or a portrait of Hitler in the house? Hitler's book was required reading for every German family.

Father's absence was discussed very little during the weeks he was gone, and this mystery lay like a dark cloud over all of us. Years later, when I was an adult, I asked about my father's disappearance and was given conflicting stories. Fräulein von Voigt, in a letter, explained it this way: "Your father was sent to a camp to train for the *Volkssturm* (People's Storm, a desperation draft of boys and old men). But to both your mother's and to my own relief, he was released in a few weeks. He came home just in time for Christmas."

My mother's explanation, on the other hand, indicated that the *Volkssturm* had been a cover story. Father's disappearance, she said, had been political. "Paps was put into a political camp, not a military one, "she said. "He refused to talk about it. But I believe that the SS was trying to force him to join the party. He was treated very badly. Food, sleep and cigarettes were withheld. He was accused of being 'an enemy of the state.' "

I have no explanation for the equally mysterious reappearance of my father. He was just in his office one day when I came back from school. I have no idea how he got out of his camp. It is possible that the collapsing eastern front forced the closing of SS political reeducation camps in Poland in the fall of 1944. Or had my father paid a bribe?

A long time later, when we were both living in West Germany, by then the *Bundesrepublik Deutschlands* (Federal Republic of Germany), I asked my father about that incident. After a long pause, he lit a cigarette and deeply inhaled from it. "That was a long time ago, and I don't want to remember. But I was never called to join the *Volkssturm*."

While my father was still away, I was told about the Warsaw Uprising by the blacksmith. "Don't tell anybody about this. We will be killed if you do," he hissed at me in a whisper. "You Germans have killed thousands of Poles in Warsaw. Now that so many are dead, they have bombed and destroyed the city."

Uncomfortable and scared, I replied that I was not German, but was Baltic German and that my family had nothing to do with the killing in Warsaw. I did not completely believe him. And I vowed not to go to his shop again.

Soon I had a reality check, this time in a movie house I was not supposed to visit. An older girl friend, Ingegerd Hirsch, offered to take me through a side door to see a film not permitted for juveniles under fourteen. The name of the main film has escaped me, but I do remember the *Wochenschau*. It showed a group of smiling soldiers in black SS uniforms linking arms and standing in front of a large mound of rubble. Windowless buildings filled the Warsaw city street in the background. So the blacksmith had been right after all.

The Warsaw Uprising in early August of 1944 was different than the Jewish Ghetto Revolt of April 1943, but they both ended just as horribly. At the Jewish Ghetto Revolt in Warsaw 36,000 people were either killed or sent to death camps. At the Warsaw Uprising, SS Chief Heinrich Himmler declared: "We shall finish them off… Warsaw will be liquidated…" Sixty-three days later the uprising was crushed. Fifteen thousand Polish partisans had been killed, and between 200,000 and 250,000 Polish men, women and children were dead. Warsaw itself was in ruins.

These exact facts of the uprising I only learned later, of course. But the war in the fall of 1944 had entered our lives for keeps. My brother Ulf and most of the boys from his school were sent to Warsaw for several weeks in September to dig anti-tank ditches. They lived in tents without heat, still wearing their school uniforms. When they got back, Ulf and his classmates spent the next four weeks taking basic infantry training in Poznan.

"We were still wearing shorts, had only carrot soup to eat, and burned our mattresses to stay warm," he said.

Ulf was not yet back from his infantry training when I celebrated my thirteenth birthday in early November. I was allowed to invite a group of my school friends living in town. On that Sunday afternoon, we gathered around the candle-lit *Kringel,* the Swedish pretzel-shaped specialty traditional for birthdays. As soon as it turned dark, we heard the Kalisz air raid sirens. Majkow did not have a bomb shelter, only a small root cellar under the kitchen. Living three kilometers outside the city in the country, my parents felt pretty safe from air attack. But we turned off all the lights with the exception of my father's office. Here, the adults gathered to sit out the alarm in a lit room with shrouded windows. In the meantime, my birthday guests and I had the dark house to play in all to ourselves. An ordinary game of *Blinde Kuh* (hide and seek) turned into a memorable event, heightened by fears of falling bombs and the spookiness of dark rooms.

The Russian planes never came. Once the clear sirens sounded, my party guests were driven home by our coachmen.

Ulf returned in December, just in time to have his sixteenth birthday. He was likely to be drafted any day, and felt resigned to serving out of fear if not desire. "I might want to join," he told me. "I heard that if you don't, roving packs of SS will string you up on trees."

My father, after his return from camp, set quietly to work laying the groundwork for our departure under the guise of preparing for Christmas. He found a black market source for textiles. Though he was reluctant to shop illegally, it offered the only way to give Christmas presents to his farm workers. Textiles and shoes were hard to get even by means of government-issued ration cards, and Polish farm workers were not even issued ration cards. Miraculously my father and Fräulein von Voigt obtained travel permits to go by train to Lódz to check out their illegal source. The care my parents tried to show towards their Polish workers revealed a lot about their awareness of the terrible hardships the general Polish population had to endure under Nazi rule.

My father and Fräulein von Voigt returned just in time for Christmas, loaded down with scarves, hats, gloves, jackets and, as I remember, aprons. They must have bought whatever they could get. And there were leather shoes in different sizes. I became flushed with excitement when I was allowed to be present as they were handed out. The grateful words and smiles are still with me now. Some of the older women tried to kiss my father's hands, but he would not let them.

Our own Christmas was restrained. My parents had offered our house and stables as a rest station for retreating German troops. Soldiers were sleeping everywhere, on sofas, beds and the golden chairs in the great hall. The overflow camped out on the floor. On Christmas Eve, we solemnly watched my father light a single blue candle on the Christmas tree. The "Blue Candle" signified the memory of Germans living in foreign lands. We had been lighting blue candles ever since coming to Poland. In a wavering voice, my mother read from the Christmas story. A few soldiers joined in when we sang the familiar Christmas songs accompanied by my mother playing the piano. There were no presents.

German party bosses and officers in the military were not allowed to discuss the exact location of the combat zone. Civilian exit was strictly controlled by the Nazis. No one could leave until receiving the official word. Neither were we allowed to make plans for it. But secretly, my parents had done just that. We were going to evacuate by horsedrawn vehicle. Thus for several nights running, once everyone had gone to bed, my parents and Fräulein von Voigt started packing from previously compiled lists. At the top of the list was the irreplaceable family silver and detailed records about family assets. The packing included warm clothing, wool blankets and provisions for us and ten horses. These crates, boxes and suitcases were piled up together with sacks of oats in the grain elevators. This preliminary work was done before the new year.

Early in the morning of New Year's Day 1945, I woke up from what I thought was the sound of machine gun fire. I got out of bed and crawled in fear and darkness to my parents' bedroom. I found them on hands and knees in their nightclothes on the floor underneath the shuttered windows. Soon the noise was followed by an awesome silence. My father stood up and peeked cautiously through a gap in the shutters. He chuckled.

"It's all right," he laughed. "We are being serenaded by the grooms. Come and take a look."

We saw a line of men silhouetted against the snow. On closer look I recognized them as our own grooms, standing like cowboys, legs spread wide. They started up again with a second salvo of cracks from their long horse whips. It really sounded like machine gun fire. Nobody had told us about the Polish New Year's Day tradition for grooms to crack the whips.

"The people must have liked their clothes," my mother said. Relieved, she rushed back to bed and disappeared under her covers. "How could I think it was an uprising?" she added. The grooms were later rewarded with money and sugar cookies.

A few days later Ulf was drafted into the Army. But he had already volunteered for the Navy. This gave my mother an excuse to see the commandant in Kalisz and plead that Ulf's draft notice be cancelled. Miraculously, it was.

"I now think that by taking this initiative, Mutti saved my life," Ulf told me later.

We finally received the official notice to evacuate on the morning of January 18. Our relief was huge. For days, rumors had circulated about the Red Army's revenge on Polish and German civilians. Rape, looting and mass executions were allegedly taking place, especially of German civilians. The bad news was that my forty-seven-year-old father and Ulf were not allowed to leave with us. Instead, the women in our family were to join a trek of others led by Baron von Ungern Sternberg, the family friend and breeder of the ill-fated mink. My father was ordered to stay and help with the organization of another trek of ethnic Germans from Bessarabia. The Bessarabian group had been resettled as farmers in and around Majkow.

My father had twenty-four hours to get his own family ready. We were to travel in four covered wagons and the enclosed coach. Four Polish grooms had agreed to drive the four wagons. My mother opted to be the driver of the coach with Grandmama and Fräulein Lukas inside. To entice the grooms away from their frightened families, my father promised that it would be just a temporary trip. The Germans would hold, he said, and then launch a new offensive that would bring them all back. There was so little real information available to the public that the story was for a time convincing. My father told me the same lie.

Bread was baked, two pigs were slaughtered, previously made sausages and hams were packed. Sacks with oats and bales of hay, together with all the already boxed family silver, warm clothing, some pails and pots were loaded. Custom-made and water-tight tarps covered the wagons. Ten of the best horses were outfitted with studs to handle icy roads. I was distressed when I heard that my pony, Max, was not among them. But my tearducts stayed dry.

In all this chaos, more fleeing soldiers arrived. They were everywhere, cooking in the kitchen, sleeping in our beds, and on the floor of the living room and my father's study. To get from one room to the next, I stepped over their death-like bodies. Floor space was at a premium for us all.

My mother took me aside. "There is something I want you to think about. Choose a small item to pack that you will remember Majkow by."

"But Mutti, you said we aren't leaving for good." I was bewildered. "You said that we'll be back soon."

"We'll be back, but I don't know when." With a slight tremor to her hand, she brushed back a strand of her hair in a familiar gesture.

My thoughts rushed from one object to the next. Should it be the scrapbook with my prized collection of *Glanzbilder* (embossed and glazed pictures of flowers, animals, and angels), my goldfish, or box of watercolors? I was desperately searching for the right thing when I overheard my father say to a German officer:

"They will never survive this, and I don't want to leave them behind. I will tie them to a tree. Then, could you shoot them? My hands are shaking too much."

He was talking about Grandmama's Putzi and our Achti. My father did not let me watch the shooting. I heard the two shots. It was over quickly. With my nose running and tears freezing on my cheeks, I helped bury their bodies in a snow bank.

Suddenly, the situation in the kitchen turned ugly. Maria came running. She was looking for my mother. "Please, Gosposa, what am I to do?" she wailed. "People are taking our food. The soldiers… and now the peasants… strangers… I don't know any of them. They're stealing everything."

The looting had started and we had not even left yet. I noticed familiar faces among the men and women who sneaked through the house. A strange man picked up one of the golden Empire chairs and vanished into the darkness of a snowy night. Where are they taking our things? I wondered. In my parents' dressing room, I found a woman grabbing as many of my mother's dresses as she could hold. When she saw me, she dropped everything and ran.

I was nervous and scared, but also excited about the eminent venture to the unknown. I believed my parents' lies that we were to return soon. Maybe the sleeping soldiers with their rifles and machine guns would see to it that we could come back. My mother's suggestion to bring something special came back into focus. I knew what to bring—the bright red winter apples.

She helped me pick them out from the fruit cellar. "You sure that's what you want to take? There might be…" She stopped in mid-sentence when we both heard the rumble of artillery not that far away. We looked out the window, and through the falling snow we could see a fiery red glow in the eastern sky. We considered the view in silence.

"Can I sit next to one of the drivers?" I asked, in my mind already on my way.

Chapter 9

My father's embrace was more gruff than tender. Grasping my shoulders, he held me for a long time. With his delphinium blue eyes he looked deep into mine: "You'll be brave now, will you?" He gave me a rough pat on the shoulder.

My brother did not want to hug. He just turned away without saying anything. So I threw myself into the arms of Maria and Lisa, who responded with solemn expressions on tear-streaked faces.

Our Polish drivers wore masks of anxiety too. They couldn't be sure that the violence approaching with the Red Army was falling only on Germans. Also, it occurred to me much later, the Poles had to have feared what liberation from Adolf Hitler by Josef Stalin might mean for their lives in the future.

It was surely hard for my parents to be separated. But I saw no tears in their eyes, just terror. They knew our family faced a special danger. Even if we escaped death in the chaos of the days ahead, my parents faced execution or deportation if captured. Their social class and Estonian origin, plus my father's fight against the Reds in 1919, marked them as counter-revolutionary Whites. Speaking Russian fluently would likely hurt rather than help. Their upper-class diction would immediately give them away.

We were now ready. The night's air vibrated with frost and distant guns. Long whiffs of misty breath streamed from the horses' nostrils. Grandmama was bundled up in her serious sable great coat, the same one she had worn during the evacuation from Estonia to Poland six years ago. The earflaps of her matching hat were

Majkow just before our departure.

tied under her chin. Regally, she and Fräulein Lukas sat on the red
leather seat inside the black coach. If it had not been for the boxes
on their laps, they both would have looked like they were going to
the opera. The boxes held Grandmama's most valued possessions:
her jewelry, a Parisian carriage clock (a gift from her father on the
occasion of her 12th birthday in 1874), and a stack of photo al-
bums recalling Grandmama's life in Avanduse. Fräulein Lukas' few
belongings were stored in one of the covered supply wagons. My
mother, their designated driver, sat on the coach box, holding the
reins for Bibi and Lola.

Bundled in overcoats much too large for me, I sat next to a
Polish driver on one of the four supply wagons. Fräulein von Voigt
was on another. We started down Majkow's snow-covered driveway
at 10:30 in the evening of January 19. At the bottom, I turned to
wave one more time to the remaining group silhouetted against the
lighted entrance of the house. The only real sadness I felt at that
moment was having to leave my pony and sheep behind. Lili was
pregnant now. Would we really be back? Who was going to look

after her? And what was going to happen to Max? Determined not to cry, I fixed my eyes straight ahead and never looked back again.

Snow was still falling when we reached the main road and joined up with Baron Ungern Sternberg, his wife, beautiful Isabella, and the rest of the trek. His familiar face reassured me. I could see a caravan of twelve horse-drawn wagons. We funneled into the right side of the road, which was packed with a single file of fleeing civilian vehicles. The left lane was taken up with faster-moving columns of German military. The military traveled by trucks, tanks, and many horse-drawn wagons. Some were on foot. Everybody was heading west. Nobody was going east.

On orders from officials of the *Nationalsozialistische Volks-wohlfahrt*, or NSV (National Socialist People's Welfare Organization), we were to drive through the night and most of the following day before taking a break. Baron Ungern Sternberg was told not to deviate from the main road to Leszno, the next checkpoint, about 80 miles (130 kilometers) away.

Between my knees was the basket with red apples. My plan was to share them for breakfast with the driver next to me. But lulled by the monotonous sound of wheels crunching on freshly fallen snow, I soon fell asleep. When I woke up, it had stopped snowing. Blinding first rays of sun glistened on frozen and snowy white fields. I looked around and saw that our five vehicles were still following each other. Our horses were still putting one foot in front of the other. The exodus of military and civilians still snaked through the flat, rural landscape. There was not a house in sight. Only the telephone poles pointed to signs of some life. Groggy and cold, I asked the driver what time it was. He shook his head indifferently, not answering. Most likely he had never owned a watch. Still resting in my lap was the basket with apples. Gone was their shiny red skin. The freezing night had turned them into a black, shriveled mess. Disgusted, I tossed the basket to the side of the road.

At noon, the baron led our caravan off the road and into a deserted farm. The house and stables had been stripped of all furnishings and equipment. A few cows stood in the snow, mooing in pain for not having been milked.

"We can't take much time here," Mother said, helping the drivers unhitch the horses. "They'll have to get fed and watered. Then we'll need to move on."

Fräulein von Voigt was already milking the cows. For one who had grown up in a city, she had caught on fast. Fräulein Lukas sawed away with a big knife in an effort to cut slices from a frozen loaf of bread. Her head trembled vigorously as she spread cold butter on the frozen slice and took a bite. The head calmed after she slurped some warm milk from the common pail.

As soon as we were back on the highway, my brooding driver spoke for the first time. "The situation is not good for us Poles. I don't know how much longer we can stick with you. We need to be with our families."

The sound of guns rumbled at our backs all day. At dusk, my mother noticed our horses' heads were sagging. Other treks had already pulled off. We were alone in the civilian lane. Baron Ungern Sternberg shouted something. His voice was drowned out by the roar of a passing military truck. We slogged into a small town. The sky was nearly black when the baron waved us through a big gate leading into a large estate courtyard.

"We'll stop there," he shouted.

A mass of refugees, wagons and horses were already milling around in the shadows. Women carried buckets of water and huge bales of hay. We managed to tuck all our wagons into parking spaces. The baron, my mother and I walked up to the open front door of Orla, the fully lit mansion. A man in riding boots, fur coat and hat emerged and greeted us in German.

"I'm not the owner. He's already left. Stay if you can find a place, but I wouldn't advise it. The Russians will be here soon." He bowed towards my mother with an elegant sweep of his hand. "There's nothing more I can do for you," he added. "I'm leaving right now." Then he stepped into the darkness.

We stayed. All of us, especially our horses, needed the rest.
Our drivers found quarters with Polish peasants in the village.
When my mother produced some smoked ham and dried peas, a
Polish woman promised to make soup for all of us and her own
family as well. She was so overjoyed that I wondered when she had
last had a decent meal herself.

The mansion itself had been completely looted days ago.
There was no furniture left, except a dirty bed in a maid's room.
My mother immediately requisitioned it for Grandmama. The rest
of us found space among the many sleeping and snoring refugees
on the straw-covered parquet floor.

On her own search for a place to sleep, Fräulein von Voigt discovered hot water in the luxuriously white-tiled master bathroom.

"I'm taking a hot bath," she whispered to me. "Would you like
to join me? It might be our last. Who knows?"

Flushed with excitement, I eagerly accepted the offer. Taking
part in such an extravagance at a time like this filled me with rapture. I easily forgot our danger. I can't remember anything about
the actual bath, just Fräulein von Voigt and I sharing the delicious
tub in a steam-filled room.

I slept profoundly, but it was still dark when I heard my
mother's voice: "Wake up! Wake up! We've got a problem. The
drivers are gone."

She had made the discovery at dawn when she had gone to
help feed and water the animals. She found two horses and one
supply wagon gone. It had held food for us and oats for the horses.
Miraculously, nothing else was missing. No drivers were in sight.
They'd headed home to protect their families.

Mother understood, and got straight to business. "We have to
repack and get out of here by ourselves as quickly as we can," she
ordered. "The baron can't wait for us. He doesn't want to risk the
entire trek." Mother held her forehead, indicating the beginning of
a migraine.

Mother and Fräulein von Voigt worked swiftly. I pitched in

when I could. We sorted and reloaded provisions for us and four horses into a single supply wagon. Grandmama and Fräulein Lukas were to stay in the coach. Two wagons and four horses were to be abandoned. We found no room for the trunks filled with family silver, handcrafted in St. Petersburg in the 1800s. I remember heaving these out of the wagon that we were taking and dumping them down in the courtyard. The only silver that we took was a baroque tea and coffee service belonging to my mother's sister, Mary. She had given it to my mother for safekeeping. It had always been referred to as the "boobs" silver because of the bare-breasted female figures carved in high relief on the handles of the bowls and pitchers.

"Mary entrusted her silver to me," my mother said. "I can't leave it here."

Once we got to the highway, we found it surprisingly empty. The rumor at Orla when we left had now put the pursuing Red Army ten miles or less to the north and south of us. We were in danger of encirclement. Our rested horses stepped out willingly, and by noon we had caught up with the tail of the refugee caravan. Baron Ungern Sternberg and our trek were only a little ahead.

In the afternoon of the third or fourth day, traffic came to a complete stop. We were about ten miles from Leszno. Even the gunfire had stopped. An eerie silence settled over the German military column and the refugees on foot or in wagons.

"We all have a pretty good chance of getting killed," one soldier said. He sat in an army truck, eyes level with my mother and me.

We sat quietly and waited. Some soldiers were sleeping. After an hour, my mother and Fräulein von Voigt decided to explore a nearby house for fresh water. They ran with empty buckets, then walked back slowly, not to spill. The horses instantly drained the buckets, wanting more. Other refugees followed. Then we waited again. Nothing moved. The eerie silence continued. Our horses were napping, their heads hanging low. Fräulein Lukas broke the silence.

"Well! What's happening?" She opened the coach's door.

Then came the planes. The noise! My mother leaped from the driver's seat screaming, "Into the ditch!"

I don't remember how I jumped, but I do remember lying in the snow, amazed to see Grandmama and Fräulein Lukas there as well. They'd made it almost as quickly as I.

The single-engine biplanes, called Red Ivans, flew so slowly they seemed to almost float above us. From the rear cockpit of each a machine gun sprayed bullets onto the crowded highway. One plane flew so low that I saw the red star on the pilot's collar tabs. In seconds they disappeared, leaving panic behind. Horses had gone wild, flipping their wagons into the ditch. Soldiers rushed about with stretchers. I saw the first dead in my life. Three bodies. Just bundles of clothes, arms askew, in the snow. I felt nothing about them. They were strangers. I was relieved that nothing had happened to us. Our horses stood in their traces, too tired to panic.

In front of us, a soldier put his rifle to the head of a mortally wounded horse. One startling shot. Then he helped the owner, a woman, drag the heavy body off the icy, highly crowned road. It left a bright stain of blood in the dirty snow. The woman was lucky to have one horse left. Her wagon was heaped with bundles, among which sat three small children, and no man in sight. Again I felt nothing.

More waiting. Dusk turned into night before the military and refugee columns started up again, each at its own pace.

"Lucky one more time," the soldier in the truck next to us said to my mother. "Our men must have broken through up ahead." He saluted, hand to helmet rim, and drove ahead.

The sky was moonless and masked with low cloud. It looked and smelled like more snow. Wagons were turning off the road, seeking shelter in empty farms for the night. Our orders were to report to a NSV refugee registration center in Leszno, and Mother was determined to get there before stopping, although she had no idea how far this might be.

"Maybe we'll have some news there from Paps and Ulf," she said.

I grew increasingly cold, hungry and tired. For the first time on the trek, I was overcome by hopelessness, despair. We were doomed. Mother noticed me shivering. "Get down and walk beside the horses," she said. "You'll stay warmer that way."

I'd taken only a few reluctant steps when I noticed that Lola and Bibi were trembling, struggling in their harnesses. The next instant, they stopped. Mother sprang from the box, rushed to Bibi, and began stroking her neck, trying to coax her forward.

"Come on, woman, move!" came an angry voice from behind.

Mother took Bibi by the bridle and tugged her forward. Powerless to resist, Lola went along. Both horses let themselves be dragged a few yards, then stopped again.

"Sigrid, help me!" she hissed. "We've got to go on."

With all my might I leaned into Lola's trembling side, pleading with her to take more steps. Mother pushed and cajoled Bibi. They finally lurched forward. We plodded along, our shoulders in the animal's flanks. Step after step. I reached exhaustion beyond tiredness—emptiness. The deep soft snow on the roadside tempted me to lie down. I heard my own voice repeating, "Go, move, go, move." Minutes. Then hours. I'm sure I wasn't supporting Lola anymore. She was now dragging me, my hands clinging to her harness, my shoulder in her side.

Around midnight, we saw lights ahead of us in the distance. Could they be Leszno?

Chapter 10

"There's no news from Paps," my mother said. She had returned to us in the Leszno courtyard, where we had rested the last few hours of the night. Mother looked worn out; she had visibly aged. "That information center was overrun by screamers. Just hysteria." We huddled close around her in the cold to hear her anxious voice.

"We have to leave at once," she added. "The man behind the desk said to get over the Oder as quickly as possible. The bridge in Glogow will be blown up—and soon."

Mother did not have to explain. In our area, the Oder River was the old border between Poland and Germany. To slow the Red Army, the Germans planned to destroy the bridges. This would give them time, however borrowed, to set up defense posts on the German side.

"But our poor horses, they're exhausted. And so am I," Fräulein Lukas said.

"The horses will manage and so will you," Grandmama assured her companion. "You and I will walk, to lighten their load."

Fräulein Lukas' head began to tremor. It always did when she felt stressed. "Whatever I say is never appreciated."

Walking was not the best idea for me. I was still missing the heel of one boot, and my socks were wet from walking in the snow the day before.

Fräulein von Voigt drove the wagon, but the rest of us trudged up the lane beside the horses and Grandmama's empty coach. By the time we reached the main road, the skies had changed from clear to overcast. It smelled of snow. The highway was packed with motorized military and civilians in wagons and on foot. Everyone jostled for a position to get ahead. Nobody wanted to make room for us. Once we did wedge in, we moved slowly and intermittently. Stop and go, stop and go. Tensions multiplied. The artillery rumbling back there—was it closer or farther away? It started to snow. I had gotten used to the sight of dead horses and abandoned wagons lining the highway. But now the big fluffy flakes quietly covered the carcasses and forsaken vehicles with little blankets of white. So long as those are not ours, I thought. Our horses' heads hung low, their scruffy flanks sunken from overwork. As I walked alongside Bibi, a feeling grew that this wonderful mare, which had been Mother's riding partner, was not going to make it. Well, no matter. Despite our gloom, we and the hundreds and thousands of other refugees on our route plodded ever to the west.

At thirteen, I was ignorant of anything not happening on this little stretch of icy road. Only later did I understand that my family's escape that winter was a tiny part of a gigantic flow of peoples out of Eastern Europe. Millions of other ethnic Germans, East Prussians, White Russians, people from the Baltics, Romanians, Tartars, Chechens, Poles, people from near the Volga River, Ukraine and Bulgaria—plus a dozen other nationalities—were in motion to the west. Many escaped, but many did not. They drowned on ships in the Baltic and fell through the ice while crossing the Baltic Sea in Masuria. Others lived and died as refugees on hundreds of highways and train routes stretching from the shores of the Baltic south through Poland, Germany, Czechoslovakia, Bulgaria, Romania, Hungary and Austria down into Yugoslavia and Greece. Immediately after the war, another 9 or 10 million, mostly Germans, but also Jews, Poles, Czechs and other nationalities, were expelled as foreign elements by newly reconstituted Eastern nations and governments. Many hundreds of thousands if not millions of these died en route, according to later census counts.

Even so, those of us who were fleeing on the roads before the advancing Red Army that winter were the lucky ones. We at least had a chance. In the annihilation camps around our wagon trains, the SS was completing its ghastly extermination of six million helpless Jews, gypsies and other victim groups. When the Red Army approached those camps, the SS deliberately shot or froze and starved their final victims by driving them along in horrid forced marches on the wintry roads.

I saw none of this. And I didn't feel at all lucky as we crawled towards Glogów and our bridge. The two-lane highway grew even more congested. Silently we worried during ever-longer stops. Would we still make it? Would the Russian army descend on the road's unprotected flanks? As afternoon turned to evening, visibility grew poorer. The road became extremely slippery with the fresh snow on old ice.

When it happened, it did so in an instant. On a downhill curve, August and Gerda lost their holds on the hidden ice surface. Without the strength to stem their slide, the horses, dragging their wagon—and Fräulein von Voigt—slipped sideways in slow motion. Gently, they all came to rest in the deep ditch. Snow came up to the axles, and August and Gerda were up to their bellies. They looked strangely peaceful and made no effort to get out. Fräulein von Voigt jumped off and was now up to her thighs in snow.

The coach, with Grandmama and Fräulein Lukas now inside, immediately stopped, causing a chain reaction among the wagons behind. The headlights of trucks shone eerily on the military units and the civilians on foot, who were the only ones still moving past us.

My mother stepped into the headlights of their traffic in a desperate effort to attract attention. She appeared as a silhouette, waving her arms like a windmill, trying to flag somebody down. Truck after tank rolled past, some barely missing her. Minutes seemed like hours. Seeing her standing there, desperate and alone, I was filled with despair. The end was here. Nobody will help us. The bridge will be dynamited. We'll never make it across the river.

We'll all be raped or killed by soldiers of the Red Army.

A rising wind drove the snow horizontally—a full blizzard. Then the miracle happened. A commanding figure on horseback stopped. He wore a German uniform and a snow-covered karakul hat pulled deeply over his face. His horse was scruffy but full of fresh energy. A machine gun hung diagonally over his shoulder. Gallantly, he raised his gloved hand in a salute.

"*Gnädige Frau* (My lady), are you in trouble? What can I do to help?" His German was heavily accented.

Mother pointed toward the ditched wagon. "Please, please, help us! We can't get out alone."

He turned in the saddle and flagged down a military truck. He commanded a unit made up of non-Germans fighting on the German side. Soldiers suddenly appeared out of the snowstorm. Shouting in an unfamiliar tongue, they worked swiftly. They freed the horses from the wagon, and with the help of a truck and heavy chains pulled it back to the road. By now some civilians had also pitched in. They and the soldiers helped us hitch August and Gerda back up again. Nothing was broken, and the harnesses remained intact. As a final gesture of gallantry, the colonel assigned two of his armed men to assist with our driving.

"We will proceed together," he shouted. "The ladies are under our protection."

Exhausted and frozen to the bone, I climbed into the coach. Nobody spoke except Grandmama.

"*Gott hilf uns,*" (God help us) she whispered, again and again.

We listened to the sounds of our own receding fears. My heart was beating so loudly I was sure Fräulein Lukas and Grandmama could hear it. Grandmama's carriage clock ticked away on her lap. We were so close now. So close. When we finally came to the bridge, I didn't see it. Swirling snow completely obscured the steel structure. I only heard the sound of hooves echoing on the bridge way. We're crossing! We're crossing! I held my breath, gasped for air and held my breath again. I pressed my hands together and silently prayed:

"Please, God, oh please, let us make it across. Don't let it blow up. Please, please, let us make it."

And we did. Magically, the sound of hooves lost their echo. I still could see nothing in the swirling snow. But the horses were

Me on rebuilt bridge over the Oder at Głogów, 1987.

clomping on solid ground. Relief to the tension came in a flood of tears. I could not stop. Grandmama gave me her linen handkerchief. God must have heard my prayers, I thought. I cried that I was alive after all. I cried, in happiness for the survival of Mother and Fräulein von Voigt. I cried, for our brave horses. And then I cried, remembering my left-behind pony, my beloved Max. I was still crying when the Hungarian colonel reappeared. He reined his horse next to Mother, who sat on the driver's box with her supposed protector, the soldier, sleeping in her lap.

He smiled at the young man. "He's just a boy, orphaned," the colonel said. "For now the danger's passed," he continued. "I have quarters for you all. You'll be my guests."

True to his word, we were led to a fully lit but empty house. It had a courtyard for our vehicles and a small stable, big enough for our horses. Silently the boy soldier fed and watered them. He showed experience. Before he vanished into the night, I had a good look at him. His slanted eyes were dull in a beardless and pockmarked face. What really caught my eye was his uniform. The filthy military coat, much too big for his lean frame, looked more Soviet than German. The original epaulets, torn away, left gaping holes on both shoulders. A large karakul hat covered his ears and head right down to the eyebrows. His feet were wrapped in dirty rags visible above tattered gray Valenkies, the felt snow boots worn alike by Russian royalty and peasants in the country. In his belt he carried a service revolver, and his shoulder held a machine gun. My mother was certain that he was a Tartar, because of his slanted eyes, she said.

Germany's initial victories left it with staggering numbers of Soviet prisoners—five million in all. Hitler decided to free prisoners who would take up arms against the Soviets. The NSV, which my mother first encountered in Leszno, set up *Ostlegionen* (Eastern Legions) made up primarily of non-Russian minorities eager to pay Stalin back for decades of oppression. Up to a million soldiers took up Hitler's offer. Among them were Tartars, Turks, Georgians, Azerbaijanis, Ukrainians and Armenians.

We discovered the ashes in the wood stove of the kitchen to be still warm. The family must have left only hours ago with nothing but the clothes on their backs. Everything was still there, including split wood to restart the fire. But it never had to come to that. The boy soldier reappeared, this time without his gun. Instead he carried an iron pot filled with steaming soup. His face remained emotionless. He left without saying a word.

We fell upon the hot soup, rich with beans and bacon. Even Grandmama joined in the slurping and smacking while eating from the common pot.

"My prayers to the Lord were answered," she said. "Erika and Fräulein von Voigt saved us again, but the Lord sent us the Hungarian gentleman."

"If there is no God, at least there is luck," remarked Fräulein von Voigt.

Fräulein Lukas' head started to shake again. "It would be nice if my prayers were appreciated too."

My mother revisited her last hour on the road. She said that soon after we began moving again, she noticed her boy soldier nodding off while holding the reins. Cold, hungry and exhausted herself, she thought that a little schnapps might help. She kept a bottle for a time just like this. She took a drink, then passed it to him. He tipped his head back and drained the bottle. Minutes later he collapsed into her lap, sound asleep.

"The soldier was about Ulf's age," she said. "I wrapped us both in my blanket and took over the reins."

I slept like a stone. But others didn't.

"Did you hear the explosion last night?" Fräulein von Voigt asked the next morning. "Just after midnight? I'm sure it was the bridge." That would have been a few hours after we crossed, I thought. I wondered if there had been anybody on the bridge when it blew. A report circulated later that there had been no warning. When the bridge blew, everyone went with it, military and civilians alike.

"Let us thank God that we are still alive," Grandmama said solemnly.

My family was never particularly religious, but we closed our eyes and bent our heads:

"The Lord is my shepherd; I shall not want…

Yea, though I walk through the valley of the shadow of death, I will fear no evil:

For thou art with me…"

My mother continued by thanking God for giving her strength to get us over the river and prayed that my father and Ulf were still alive. And she prayed that our brave horses would continue to show the strength to bring us to safety. She was interrupted by the sudden reappearance of our charismatic protector. The Hungarian colonel had come to say goodbye.

"I have orders to go south," he said, "but you can stay where you are and have some rest. It was my pleasure to meet you and maybe…maybe we'll meet again. The circumstances? Who knows?" He looked into my mother's eyes and kissed her hand. She blushed slightly, confused by his gallantry.

"We said a prayer for your safety this morning. We owe you our lives." Mother had quickly regained her composure.

Without his help we might never have made it. Nor would we have been able to find quarters on the German side of the river. Every house, stable, shed was occupied by German military. They were there to stem the offensive of the Red Army. All other civilians who had made it across the bridge were ordered to move on. I accompanied Mother on the walk to the refugee checkpoint. A Nazi party organization, the *National Socialistche Volkswohlfahrt* (National Socialist People's Welfare), was managing this and all other refugee control centers. They were fanatically efficient.

"I have no information about your husband," the NSV official said. "You'll have to go to the Droskau control point. All DPs (Displaced Persons) from Kalisz are to check in there. If your husband's alive, you'll find news of him there." Then he stepped back, raised his arm and shouted, "*Sieg Heil!* We will win the war! *Sieg Hitler!*"

Dumbfounded, neither my mother nor I responded.

After a family caucus and a discussion with German soldiers about our safety, Mother decided to stay one more day. The horses needed rest and we looked forward to sleeping one more night in clean sheets in a real bed. The house had plenty of food. The cellar supplied potatoes and turnips, and we splurged on a jar with canned white asparagus.

"The taste of these asparagus reminds me of the best cook I ever had in Avanduse," Grandmama said. "There was only one problem; he was addicted to the bottle. He spent all his earnings—and I paid him well—in the roadhouse drinking. Unfortunately, I had to let this good man go when he showed up for the morning menu planning session wearing nothing but two aprons. One tied around the front and the other around his back. The night before, he had paid with his clothes for a last drink of schnapps."

For the first time in days, I felt safe, protected by the heavy German military presence. But the highlight of that day was a pair of leather boots I found in a closet. They were men's boots, too big for me. But they had heels and a strong sole. With two pairs of men's wool socks, they fit just fine.

When Mother discovered my new footwear, she was not happy.

"That is stealing," she said deliberately. "Please put them back where they came from. I'm sure that the man of the household will miss his boots when he returns. We are only guests here. You wouldn't think of doing this in anybody else's house, now, would you?"

I pleaded and begged, showing her my old boots. So, after further thought, she reluctantly allowed me to keep the new gear.

"I'm just exchanging them," I said to make her feel better. "I'll leave my old ones where I found these."

In the meantime, where were my father and my brother? We hoped and prayed that they were alive and safe somewhere behind us. But had they made any bridge over the river? Father's diary tells their story. His and Ulf's last hours awaiting permission to leave Majkow were dicey. The SS ordered them to help evacuate a group of ethnic Germans from Bessarabia. The people were just arriving, mostly on foot, carrying rucksacks, pushing garden carts and baby carriages through the snow. A few families had carts pulled by oxen. The skins on their haunches hung in bloody shreds from having been beaten to hurry up. Everybody was in a panic to catch the supposedly last train leaving Kalisz. Father and Ulf got them loaded on board.

Among the few Poles who had already fled was our farm manager, Kerinski, and his young family. They vanished the night before we women left, fearing for their lives. Kerinsky was hated by his countrymen for his cruelty.

When my father was finally permitted to leave, the only horses remaining were my pony Max and Zapa, a skinny white Russian mare. The mare was pregnant when she came to us as war booty. Twenty-four hours before Father's departure, she gave birth to a black foal. Father hitched up Max and Zapa and left the foal behind. All other horses had been stolen. Most of the cattle had vanished overnight too, and so had the pigs and chickens. The house itself was being looted of all furniture and rugs as Father made his own preparations. The pantries had long been emptied.

"Every man for himself," the SS commandant told my father before fleeing himself. "There'll be no military protection. The enemy is very close—ten miles from where we stand."

Stored on his wagon was the magnificent family collection of English silver-inlaid hunting guns and two crates packed with oil paintings, separated only by sheets of butcher paper. Frames and stretchers had been removed. Besides sacks of oats, my father brought food for himself and Ulf. The smoked ham, bacon, dried beans and bag of flour had come from a cache he had hidden under his bed. He did not forget his bicycle and beloved Zeiss microscope. The Zeiss, a present from my grandparents for his fourteenth birthday, had survived World War I and the following revolutionary upheavals, and Father was not going to leave it behind now. The wagon was covered by a watertight tarp. Armed with two pistols and detailed military maps of the region, he and Ulf started out before midnight on January 20, the day after we did.

From the start, Father decided their best chance at escape lay in avoiding the clogged main highway leading west. With the help of his maps, he traveled on small country roads. At times, huge snow banks slowed them—the roads weren't cleared. But the decision to break free and detour around the fleeing crowds and columns of military most likely saved their lives. They changed direction several times to avoid being caught by the Soviet army. But they were never stopped by traffic jams, nor were they strafed by Red Ivans. Father avoided all refugee checkpoints too. He was afraid that the SS might grab Ulf and put him under arms. They spent nights under cover in deserted farmhouses.

At one intersection Father ran into a trek with people originally from Bessarabia. In conversation, their leader mentioned witnessing the murder of a Polish farm manager.

"To me it looked like an act of revenge, done by people who knew him or about him," the man said. "It happened so fast—the man had no time to pull his gun. They stabbed him many times. His wife and child were spared. They left them alone after they took his horses and gun. Who knows what he had done to be killed by his own people."

Listening to the tale, father asked a few questions and realized that the man who was killed was none other than Kerinski. His former farm manager had apparently been pursued and ambushed by men from Majkow. Father was shocked. He knew Kerinski had grown unpopular but had no idea that he was so hated. These same workers had been polite and helpful in seeing us off.

Just seven days out of Majkow, Father and my brother, two exhausted ponies and their wagon reached the Oder River. They crossed on a bridge to the north at Zielona Gora. Once on the other side, father learned of the Droskau checkpoint for DPs from Kalisz. Droskau was a mere 28 miles away, a two- or three-day drive under relaxed conditions behind German lines. They arrived January 30, but found no word of us. More refugees were coming in every day, they were told, so they settled into a room within two blocks of a stable for Zapa and Max.

The next day, my father was lucky to locate and buy some feed. He was walking slowly down the main road through town, a fifty-pound sack of oats on his shoulder, when suddenly he heard a familiar feminine voice from behind:

"Billchik, is this you?" My father turned to see my beaming mother. We had just been entering town. I was sitting on the coach box with her when she suddenly tensed and waved her hand toward a figure up the street.

"You see that man up there, the one carrying the sack?" she asked. "Don't you think he looks like Paps?"

The suddenness with which we had so easily found each other left us stunned. It took me half a minute or more to grasp the reality of my father standing in front of me, alive and well. But my next thought was, how had he managed to get here before us? It seemed strangely unfair.

Mother jumped from the coach. My parents embraced, my father kissed her hand. "But where's Ulf?"

"He's with Max and Zapa."

I could not believe my ears. "Maxi? Maxi's here? Where?"

Grandmama and Fräulein Lukas emerged from the cocoon of their coach blankets. We all were standing in the middle of the street, talking and blocking traffic.

"I'm taking them feed. They're just down the road. Want to come?" Father asked.

I had not touched my diary for weeks. But that night I wrote in the tiny space for January 31: "We met Paps on the street. How lucky we are that he is alive. My dear Maxi came with him!!! Glorious!!! It's a good time but not a good time. Mutti has a migraine."

When I met Ulf, I asked him if the experience on his trek had been scary.

"Oh no, it was a great adventure," he said.

Sixty years later a memoir appeared in Canada underlining how lucky we had been. Fred Bruemmer, in *Survival, a Refugee's Life,* published by Key Porter Books in 2005, writes that his family, Baltic Germans like ourselves, fled an estate near Kalisz the same day we did, January 19. At most they could have been only a few miles behind us women. And my father and Ulf had started a day later. Five days out from Kalisz, advancing Soviet tanks brushed the Bruemmers off the road into a field, where they were collected and marched to a jail. The adults were all shot out of hand. Fred Bruemmer, then fifteen, was dispatched in a cattle car to a forced labor camp in southern Russia.

The NSV office picked my father to lead a group of DPs further into Germany. There were forty-eight ethnic German families who had originally come from the Ukraine, Hungary, Czechoslovakia, and Bessarabia. Father spent days in Droskau getting everybody organized. They needed to be registered, issued passports and ration cards. Some had medical problems. I was overwhelmed by the various languages spoken, but my father managed with a mixture of Ukrainian, Russian and German. Food was a constant problem—the lean years had begun in earnest. One family had had a grandmother die on the road a whole week earlier. In their rush to get over the bridge, they'd had no time to bury her. Besides, the ground was frozen hard. Now she lay peacefully frozen next to

bundles of clothes and sacks of oats on their cart. Father found a
cemetery, but where, near the front lines, do you find gravediggers
willing to work in frozen soil? All able-bodied young and even
middle-aged men were either still at war or had already been killed.
Eventually, Father, with the help of the NSV, rounded up a team
of old men who scraped out a shallow hole.

On February 9, my father was given his route. Our trek was
headed to the Halle/Merseburg region deep in Saxony (map). Our
final destination, he was told, would be assigned later. We immediately encountered an endless traffic jam. Father persuaded the
Droskau refugee commander to reroute us via smaller routes further north, towards Cottbus. Daytime progress became fairly easy.
Our horses were rested, a thaw had set in, and the Russian air force
left us alone. For the first time, Father's bicycle came in handy. Each
day he pedaled ahead to secure overnight accommodations for his
small army of people—roughly two hundred and their horses.
Much to his surprise, he encountered outspoken hostility. Nobody
was interested in hosting that many people and horses even for just
one night. The locals, Father wrote, called our group of DPs "a
bunch of desperate gypsies. Who knows where they come from

The trek in Germany: I am driving Max and Zapa on my father's
wagon. Ulf alongside; Kaspar Ludwar, trek assistant, in front.

...they can't even speak proper German. Their women and children are filthy, infested with lice. They will steal our last chicken... they'll rob us blind."

With difficulty, and great diplomacy, Father convinced the village mayors to take us in. Only once did he fail. The mayor of Grötsch, between Cottbus and Wittenberg, refused to put us up. In pouring rain, our caravan waited outside the village limits. Hours passed and it turned dark before Father came back to give us the bad news. We covered the horses with tarps and kept some for ourselves. I was allowed to spend the night sitting up with Grandmama and Fräulein Lukas inside the coach, worrying about Max catching pneumonia outside. I could not sleep because of the sound of rain on the coach roof and the ticking of Grandmama's carriage clock. She and Fräulein Lukas had an argument about something that I cannot remember. But I do remember Fräulein Lukas saying what-she said so many times: "I'm not appreciated anymore by anybody."

Father wrote in his diary:

> After this most sleepless of nights, we found a welcoming refuge the next night in Ogrosen. The villagers opened their hearts and houses. They turned the *Gasthaus* into a refugee warehouse. We were treated to a hot meal—first one in days.

We pushed further west, taking our time. Food was increasingly scarce, but the front had temporarily stabilized on the Oder. The crunch of artillery to our rear was a memory. We crossed and re-crossed the Elbe River several times, passing through Finsterwalde, Herzberg, Tröbitz and Holzdorf. The attitudes of the German population improved. Village mayors turned helpful. Father bicycled back from the town of Düben with the news that he had been given the names of two villages, Salzfurtkapelle and Wadendorf, as permanent places to stay. They were only a couple of days away. The faces of every family lit up; they chattered happily in half a dozen tongues. To celebrate, Father offered everyone roll-your-own cigarettes from his stash of homegrown tobacco. I will never forget the rapture on their faces after inhaling the first puffs of the prized luxury.

My father's entry on February 19:

> We pulled into Salzfurtkapelle exactly a month after the day we left Majkow. Forty-seven families had come that far. Only one family stayed behind when their horses gave out. But even they showed up a few days later. With the help of the local organization in charge of settling DPs, every family found a roof over their heads and a stable for their horses. I cannot express with words the accomplishment I felt of bringing that many people to safety.

We were now refugees in a strange place. The war was still on. But we were deep inside Germany. Russian troops might still occupy our village. But amid all our uncertainty, we felt that for the moment at least we had escaped the very worst. We were then only vaguely aware of the disaster that had befallen virtually all those German refugees who were overrun on the road by the combat units of the advancing Red Army. John Erickson of the University of Edinburgh, in *The Road to Berlin*, published by Harper & Row in 1983, is fully sympathetic to Russian suffering at the hands of the Nazis, but describes the Red Army's entry into the eastern provinces of Germany this way:

> Speed, frenzy and savagery characterized the advance. Villages and small towns burned, while Soviet soldiers raped at will and wreaked an atavistic vengeance in those houses and homes decked out with any of the insignia or symbols of Nazism...some fussily bedecked Nazi Party portrait photograph would be the signal to mow down the entire family amidst their tables, chairs and kitchenware. Columns of refugees, combined with groups of Allied prisoners uprooted from their camps and slave labor no longer enslaved in farm or factory, trudged on foot or rode in farm carts,

some to be charged down or crushed in a bloody smear of humans and horses by the juggernaut Soviet tank columns racing ahead with assault infantry astride the T-34s...Under the lowering January skies and the gloom of late winter, families huddled in ditches or by the roadside, fathers intent on shooting their own children or waiting whimpering for what seemed to be the wrath of God to pass. The Soviet Front command finally intervened, with an order insisting on the restoration of military discipline and the implementation of "norms of conduct" toward the enemy population. But this elemental tide surged on...

In other words, the fate of the Bruemmer family was the rule, not the exception, on the winter roads of eastern Europe and Germany in the first months of 1945.

Once in Salzfurtkapelle, we were assigned the dining room and tiny butler's pantry in the manor house of Salzfurtkapelle's demesne. Other refugees were already there, sharing the large country kitchen with the ill-disposed owners. I was helping my mother wash the dishes when I overheard Frau Osterland complain to her husband:

"Can't you stop this invasion? We can't feed any more of these people. And they trash our house. It's our house, isn't it?"

He shrugged. "We'll do what the Party wants."

Father found bales of clean straw to use as bedding for us and our six horses. The first few nights we slept on the floor, grateful to have one and a half rooms. The sounds of wheels crunching on snow had passed. Early spring, bringing warmer temperatures, had finally arrived.

Days later, a carpenter built crude wooden platform beds so that we could sleep on straw-filled mattresses stitched together from linen sheets. But we still could not sleep through the nights. Hunger kept us wakeful. Ration cards were useless. The stores were empty, shuttered tight. Fräulein von Voigt and Mother got jobs mucking out in the diary barn in exchange for a pitcher of fresh milk twice a day. Father traded August and Gerda for flour, oatmeal, a few eggs and pickled pork. It was a hard, tearful decision to make. Horses used for personal transport in pre-automotive times became part of one's family. And these horses, pulling the supply wagon, had saved our lives. Not just them, but also the other four. Eventually, they all went on the swap block for food.

We grew desperate for anything edible. When the first greens appeared in the wild in March, Mother collected fresh dandelion leaves and early sprouts of nettles from which she made meal after meal of a watery soup. Grandmama came down with a bad case of dysentery. She stayed in her bed, except to rush out to one of the three outhouses sitting on the manure pile. As on many German farms, the manure pile is in the middle of the large courtyard. We and the other refugees shared the outhouses with the Russian and Polish prisoners working as forced labor on the farm. We were wary of each other, but got along.

My father wangled permission to plant a small section in the Osterlands' vegetable garden. He managed to scrounge seeds for cold weather vegetables like peas, spinach and Swiss chard. It was more than future nutrition for us. To keep his own sanity over his difficult lifetime, Father developed a philosophy of looking at life through plants, any plants. He lived, breathed and talked plants always. They could be ornamentals, vegetables or field crops. Watching them grow nourished his soul and helped him keep his balance.

Nazi propaganda from a loudspeaker in the village screamed promises of final victory at us daily. But everyone knew that the war was lost. A silent suspense settled in. Each family was absorbed in fixing something, in sewing, in waiting to cook food, in cooking food, in waiting to wash clothes, in washing clothes, in searching—always searching—for food. Ulf and I did whatever chores we could. But mostly we just hung out, waiting with everyone else. Allied airplanes roamed our skies. Our village was blacked out each sundown.

On one clear night we watched the bombing of Dessau, ten miles to the north. We marveled at the sky ablaze with sparkling lights hanging in the air. These seemingly stationary parachute flares resembled Christmas tree lights and were aptly named for them. They were there to illuminate the city to help Allied pilots with their aim. The silent flares were then joined by wave after wave of fiery salvos and tracers from German anti-aircraft guns. We were glued to our perch on an elevated spot watching the spectacle—open-mouthed and speechless.

Fräulein Lukas, coming alive amid the collapse, used the blackouts to start a romance with the widowed farm manager. He whispered to her later that he had heard that Dessau had been completely flattened, burning for days with unchecked fires. The blackouts also served as cover for German straggler soldiers looking for a place to hide. Some came out of the dark on crutches, others without shoes, walking on bloodied feet and in tattered uniforms. They pleaded for water and food. We found them hiding in the haylofts. Mother again cried a lot. When nobody was looking she brought them water and her dandelion soup.

By early April, the Russian prisoners and Polish forced laborers on the farm grew increasingly restless. Many of these gaunt men and women refused to show up for work. All demanded more food. I remember overhearing their armed German overseer, speaking in German, belittle them as "ungrateful!" The prisoners' fear of him kept them from open rebellion right to the end.

The overwhelming question on everybody's mind during these last days became, who would occupy us first? The Russians and Poles vigorously hoped it would be the Red Army. My parents cared or knew little of the Americans, who were to them a distant, non-European and therefore alien race. But the horror stories of Russian treatment of German refugees, and my parents' personal history as enemies of communism, clearly meant that they hoped for an American occupation. Mother openly expressed one practical concern: "Let's hope and pray that it will be the Americans. They will have their own supplies and will not take anything from us."

Then, on a sunny Sunday in mid-April, the American tanks

rolled in. The night before, a voice over the village loudspeaker had instructed people to stay inside, preferably in their cellars, until further notice. "The German Army will defend our village from the enemy," the anonymous voice had intoned.

But no troops that we could see arrived, and the night passed quietly. In the early morning hours, Ulf and I snuck outside and hid in an elevated gazebo. It looked over a stone wall, and we were shocked to find we had a perfect first view of the "enemy." American tanks, trucks, towed cannons and soldiers in battle gear were calmly filling the village square and streets. The German army was nowhere to be seen. We stared, I was a little scared, but we both marveled at the astounding sight of a victorious army.

We ran to our parents with the news.

Chapter 11

"The Americans are here, the Americans are here," we cried almost in unison. Within minutes, a small group of edgy armed soldiers burst in on us, shouting,

"Weapons! Give us your weapons! Your guns!"

They confronted my father first. Not speaking English, he did not understand what they said. Misunderstanding his hesitation, the soldiers screamed louder and kicked the wooden crates holding Grandmama's painting collection that my father had brought with him. The rest of us sat fully dressed on our beds, rigid, watching. Grandmama sported her sable-lined great coat, and my mother wore her silk bandana wrapped around her forehead, indicating the approach of a migraine. Fräulein Lukas' face was flushed and her head was bobbing vigorously. My father caught on eventually and eagerly pulled the two cases containing his hunting guns from underneath his wooden cot. With shaking hands, he handed them over, adding his Rolleiflex camera and the two pistols he and Ulf had brought with them on the trek. With horror we watched through a window as the soldiers carried the magnificent silver-inlaid English shotguns outside and smashed them against the trunks of the two big linden trees framing the entrance to the manor house. They pocketed the camera and two handguns and returned inside to clear the next rooms.

While we were being searched, a tank had rumbled into the wagon-crowded courtyard. More American soldiers appeared. They fanned out to surround the stables, cow barns and farm storage buildings. We heard them yell and simultaneously shoot salvoes into the air. One by one the tattered and shoeless German soldiers came out. Only twenty-four hours ago, my mother had brought them dandelion soup and water. Clasping hands behind their heads, they boarded a few waiting jeeps and were quickly whisked away.

One search team ran into trouble on the second floor of the mansion. They came upon a locked door. When it did not give to their banging and kicking, they used a machine gun to shoot out the locks. An end to that shattering noise brought people out of their rooms, crowding the hall space. I was among them, but standing in back. Eventually, after much neck craning, I had a glimpse of the dark room. What I saw left me slightly dizzy. The room was crammed with food. Stacked from floor to ceiling, I saw box after box filled with butter, cans of lard, bags of flour and sugar, some coffee, even cigarettes. The untouched butter, now mildewed and rancid, glistened through the paper wrappings of one-pound packages. How could all this food have been here, stored in the same house in which we were desperate for something to eat?

Once the soldiers convinced themselves that there were no guns and no German soldiers behind the boxes, they moved on to

American First Army arrives in a town like Salzfurtkapelle, spring 1945.

other rooms. In the confusion, a few Russian prisoners had joined us in the mansion and were now shouting for the attention of the GIs. I couldn't hear what was said next between them. But soon I saw the Osterlands in handcuffs being brought downstairs. Herr Osterland appeared in a German officer's uniform, and his wife wore a magnificent fur coat. Heads held high, they both were taken away in a jeep. We never saw them again. We were told much later that they were charged with war crimes for willfully withholding food from the prisoners who had worked their farm.

Within an hour of the arrest of the Osterlands, the bolder refugees and Russian prisoners had completely emptied the storage room. They fought over each box and basket, brandishing pitchforks and clubs. The violent scene left me so frightened that I ran empty-handed downstairs and hid in my bed. In the chaos of those first hours, I don't think that my parents had ever realized I'd been gone.

In the afternoon, we watched the liberated Russians celebrate their freedom. Glued to the windows, we saw them slaughter a pig. The pig's screams mixed with the Russians' drunken howls. Others had seized all the bicycles and rode like children around and around the courtyard. The orgy of liberty climaxed with the roasting of the pig on an open fire pit. It was all quite scary. Would we get their attention next? My parents wondered where they'd found the alcohol. Surely the American soldiers hadn't supplied it. Maybe the schnapps was part of the stash in the storage room?

As night came, the party grew even wilder. The Russians danced and sang and drank. Somebody played a harmonica in the dark. The party was occasionally punctuated by gunshots. Whose guns?

We stayed awake all night, listening and listening from our straw beds. The next day brought no relief from the tumult. Ulf and I were glued to the windows. We marveled at the Sherman tank in the courtyard. Covered trucks rolled in pulling pieces of artillery. More troops arrived. We admired the casual, confident walk of those soldiers, and enviously watched them chew gum and smoke cigarettes, sometimes both at the same time. Open packages of what we came to recognize as Camels and Lucky Strikes peeked from their uniform pockets.

We saw one of the soldiers who'd taken the Osterlands away. Today he wore Herr Osterland's officer's hat, rakishly tipped back to expose a strange brush haircut. The Russians seemed to have vanished. But we saw their German labor boss. He stepped forward out of the dairy barn alone, silhouetted against the darkness of the open doorway. With his hands in his pockets and his cap pushed back, he surveyed the courtyard as if he did not have a worry in the world. That changed abruptly when we heard a single shot. The labor boss fell backwards, coming to rest on the manure-covered floor of the barn. He was immediately surrounded by a wall of shoving GIs. We couldn't see what happened next. We didn't know that he'd died instantly, killed by a single shot through the heart, until Mother gave us the news.

"It must have been an act of revenge," she said. "Maybe one of the Russians convinced an American sharp shooter to kill him. They've been saying he was terribly cruel." We never learned who fired that shot.

At noon we were allowed to use the kitchen for the first time since the Americans had showed up thirty hours before. It was packed with refugees and soldiers, cooking, talking, shaving and eating. My father marveled, in a handwritten note at the time, that these easygoing Americans shared the kitchen with us "without the slightest friction, something that was impossible with the Osterlands." Some of the solders, still wearing their camouflaged helmets and guns, were listening to a radio they had brought. Suddenly the program seemed to be interrupted with an announcement I could not understand. The reaction was instant. More soldiers poured into the kitchen, all crowding around the radio. They looked solemn, several even damp-eyed. One covered his face and wept openly. It took a while for me to find out that Franklin Roosevelt, the American president, had died four days earlier. The soldiers were apparently hearing a memorial broadcast from his burial, which had taken place in America the afternoon before. The tears of that hardened front line soldier startled me.

In the confusion of soldiers and refugees milling about the smoky kitchen, my mother finally managed to secure a cooking space on the coal-burning stove. She produced a gray gruel from milk, rice and potato starch, which to all of us tasted like ambrosia. We had not eaten anything warm in what seems now like days. From my father's notes I much later learned that our meal came from supplies that the Osterlands had shared out before they'd been arrested.

That evening the people in Salzfurtkapelle were warned about a possible counterattack and battle. German troops had somehow reappeared and set up a defense line in Siebenhausen, a tiny village about a mile and a half east, separated from Salzfurtkapelle by the Autobahn. We were advised to spend the night in the basement. Grandmama and Fräulein Lukas refused to go to the airless, damp root cellar of the mansion. So we all stayed in our first floor room, spending another sleepless night, this time right in the middle of an artillery exchange. One of the American cannons stood just outside our windows in the courtyard. The noise was tremendous. Every few minutes another round went off. Luckily, neither our mansion nor courtyard was hit by the random German return fire. Amazingly, I was so worn by exhaustion that I actually managed to sleep a little between the outgoing rounds.

In the early morning, just when the rising sun pink-streaked the sky, Ulf and I stole up to the attic. It was his idea to see for ourselves the damage being done to Siebenhausen. We were rewarded by the dramatic sight of burning buildings and explosions of debris from shrubs, stones and the soil of the town. We heard the shells leave from our courtyard and seconds later saw them hit in Siebenhausen. Little did we know that within less than six months our family would come to live in that village and, specifically, in a farm compound that had been hit by the American guns.

The shelling stopped before noon. Nobody had been killed or injured in our village, but we later learned that four German soldiers had died defending Siebenhausen. Both settlements suffered considerable damage to their houses and farm buildings. Salzfurtkapelle's wells had been hit and contaminated. We began boiling our water. By the evening, Siebenhausen had apparently surrendered. In any case, the sounds of even small arms fighting stopped. The original American combat troops in Salzfurtkapelle pulled out shortly afterward and a different unit replaced them.

Sixty years later, rummaging through my father's papers, I opened a small lined notebook, labeled "Trek Book 1945," which held random jottings that stopped after half a dozen pages. I'd seen these entries before. But this time I flipped idly all the way through the little booklet. I was startled to find, beginning on a middle page, two entries containing my father's first impressions of our conquerors. The pages covered some of the events of the days I have just described, but we children had been confined to the mansion and courtyard. My father had seen more and characteristically reflected on it. From the first entry:

Salzfurtkapelle, the 18th of April, 1945

Three days of American occupation. The stage has revolved. We now view the world from the other side…The Americans behave calmly and correctly. They are tall athletic figures with free-swinging gaits—no rigid military bearing—the greatest possible contrast to the German military. There are no loud commands, no shouting, no blustering, no standing at attention. Orders are quietly, easily passed and quickly carried out.

These are pure tank troops, which defines the circumstances of their unique existence. Each tank is dispersed at 100 meter intervals from the others in the fields surrounding the estate. Camp life for each small group develops around their tanks. The soldiers cook, clean, sunbathe, and sleep around them. Then suddenly a soldier climbs up to a

machine gun and fires a burst of shots in the direction of
the front line. Then he climbs down, and a cozy peace reset-
tles around the tank. A strange war! Gunfire is rattling somewhere constantly in this way against an invisible front line.
There seems to be no return fire.

When the fighting for Siebenhausen ended, we returned to
our routine of searching for fresh greens in the Osterland garden
and their fields. Rumors passed that typhoid cases had appeared in
Salzfurtkapelle. I never learned if it was true—most of our news
was rumor. Ulf and I rummaged through the American garbage
cans, looking for leftovers from their "C-rations." These were
amazing cartons of canned and packaged meals which even came
with little heating canisters. In time I became friendly with some of
the soldiers, who in return offered me my first chewing gum. Eventually I became bold enough to ask for Hershey bars, wrapped in
olive-green paper as were all the C-rations. I kept the chocolates,
not even thinking of sharing them, and gave the cigarettes to my
grateful parents. For weeks I had noticed my father's nicotine with-

Americans relax around tank in occupied town, spring 1945.

drawal symptoms. He never complained, but had nervously fiddled with his cigarette paper and empty tobacco box.

Work in the dairy barn kept us from starving. I somehow remember that my mother and Fräulein von Voigt did most of the labor, but my father's notes make it clear that he pitched in too. Since the main dairy operation was temporarily shut down, all the milk and dairy products were available to the refugees on the estate and local inhabitants. People took turns milking, mucking and feeding the cows. These cows and a few pregnant pigs were all that was left of the animals. Newly born calves, ducks and all of the chicken had long been slaughtered and eaten. Most of the work horses were gone too. The Russians had hitched them up to wagons loaded with loot. Many had set off east by the end of the first week. Only Fräulein Lukas avoided the dairy barn. She spent her time holding hands with Herr Motte, the Osterlands' widowed farm manager. Grandmama was too weak to complain about the lack of attention. She now spent most of her time in bed, covered by horse blankets, suffering the after effects of dysentery.

In the midst of our struggles, my father was still thinking hard about the Americans. They seemed with their ample food supplies and easy, informal manner to be almost a different breed of human being. In his second entry, a week after the Americans arrived, he muses:

Sunday, 22nd of April, 1945
...Instead of military compulsion, a self-evident camaraderie prevails that lets the entire military organism run forward without friction, whether the solders are on duty or off and loafing around...

The support of this military is excellent, as if in peacetime, despite practically all the supplies having to be shipped from America. I could never have imagined such a thing... Everything they eat seems to come from cans... Of bread, hardly any is to be seen, and it is apparently not missed, because the men never ask us for any. They don't eat many potatoes either.

They take comfortable material existence for granted, and it produces the foundation for an entirely different mentality. If the German army had been supported by this level of well being, it would have been invincible and the entire mentality of the German people would have stood on a different plateau. The first requirement of a life of culture is absolute physical comfort and security...Whether the dazzling material situation of the American soldiers brings them to a higher spiritual level, however—that I doubt....one man is so completely like the other in equality of morals, habits of life and so on that it creates a flatness of spirit and intellect. I could be one-sided in this view because I can't talk to them...

My father's conclusion about the commonness of American culture stayed with him for the rest of his life. Some of these American supermen soon proved to be all too human in the here and now. Fräulein von Voigt mentioned one day that a soldier was watching her in the diary barn. It made her uneasy, especially when she was alone. No one in the family paid her any attention until the soldier showed up at our door of the butler's pantry in the middle of one night. Agitated and drunk, he demanded entry. My father was sleeping there on a wooden cot. Waving a flashlight in one hand and a pistol in the other, the soldier slurred his words:

"*Frau, Frau*, give me my *Frau*."

My father, dressed in his night clothes, tried to calm and persuade him to leave. From the other side of an unlocked door, we heard my father repeating:

"*Hier gibt es keine Frauen.* (There are no women here)."

The soldier's flashlight threw weird light patterns through the cracks of the door as I listened to their footsteps. I lay rigidly in my bed, expecting him to burst in any moment. Minutes passed like hours. But we were lucky again. The soldier was too drunk to find the door to our room. Eventually, my father coaxed him out of the butler's pantry through another door into a hallway. Once there, the soldier lost his purpose. He slumped down on the floor and in seconds was asleep, still holding the burning flashlight in one hand and the loaded pistol in the other. By the time we woke up the next morning, he had left. We never saw him again.

The news of Hitler's suicide in his Berlin bunker, the end of the war, and my discovery of Fräulein von Voigt's secret diary seemed to reach us in Salzfurtkapelle more or less on the same day. Her diary left a considerably bigger impact on me than either Hitler's suicide or the end of the war. My family and I were too stressed to devote much feeling to the final collapse. But Fräulein von Voigt's diary was filled with confessions of her love for my father.

Ulf and I shared room cleaning duties. While he swept the floor of straw that had escaped from our mattresses, I dusted the table tops and windowsills. Dusting Fräulein von Voigt's night stand, an upside-down wooden potato crate, I inadvertently knocked down a book. It turned out to be her diary. Out fell a picture of my father. When I tried to place it back inside, I could not help but read some of the entries. I remember the lines from April 29: "My darling prince! Despite my hunger, God blessed me with a peaceful night. My dreams were filled with our love for each other…I held you tight."

With a burning face I called Ulf to read what I had just discovered. Together we flew through love letter after love letter. We were shocked, then overcome by sorrow for our mother, and we decided that it was up to us to tell her. Only the sound of footsteps made us hastily retreat to our chores.

The next day Ulf and I met again in the garden. The purpose was to figure out how to tell Mother about our discovery. This was not easy. Naively, we were both sure that she had no idea about what was going on.

"We have to tell her," Ulf said. "We have to warn her. But how?"

Eventually it was his idea that seemed the best. We would coax her away to a quiet place, such as the carriage house, which still held the Osterlands' fleet of carriages. Nobody seemed ever to go there. It took us a couple of weeks to come up with the right moment. But eventually, the three of us sat on the black leather seats of a coach stored in the back of the carriage house. Ulf took out and read from a prepared statement. Before he could finish, though, Mother burst into tears, shaking uncontrollably.

"How did you ever find out?" she eventually whispered, her face in her hands.

We told her. She sat in silence, wiping her eyes. Neither then nor later did she ever acknowledge or deny that a relationship existed between my father and Fräulein von Voigt. Mother finally got up, took a deep breath, and walked out of the carriage house. After that day, we raised our discovery with no one. It had taken all of our courage to bring it up once. Nothing changed in our family, we just continued as we had before. Together, my father and Fräulein von Voigt tended the new vegetable garden. On the few occasions that Ulf and I helped, we exchanged glances whenever we thought we noticed signs of guarded tenderness between them. But as time wore on even our exchanged glances faded. What was to be done?

Spring was in the air. Fresh green sprouts emerged from most of the seeds that we had planted. The curly leaves of green peas were followed by seedlings of spinach, radishes, Boston lettuce, leeks and sorrel. My father had started tomato plants and green peppers in a cold frame. Soon my mother's soup contained spinach and sorrel in place of dandelions. Grandmama was slowly getting her strength back, just in time to congratulate Fräulein Lukas on her engagement to Herr Motte.

Their announcement came together with the official news that Germany had surrendered on May 8. Neither the end of the war nor Fräulein Lukas' engagement was celebrated. Our war had ended several weeks earlier, and the future was all that mattered. We wished the couple good luck and were sorry not to have a present to give. Fräulein Lukas, now in her mid-forties, looked happier than ever, but her head bobbing remained despite the arrival of good fortune.

Years later, when I worked as a photo editor for *Life* magazine in New York, I was mesmerized by a famous black and white photo. It showed an American sailor in New York's Times Square kissing a nurse, twisting her into an intense embrace, in celebration of the victorious end of the Second World War. The spontaneity and exuberance of that embrace, caught on film by *Life* photographer Alfred Eisenstaedt, was so glorious and so different from our bleakness in defeat that I am shocked by the contrast to this day. We were worn out, hungry, void of feeling. Nothing but more hardship lay ahead.

My father worried constantly now about how to make a living in a country where most of us refugees were resented. We occupied private rooms and ate scarce food in a country to which we were not born. Father was also running out of money, not that we could buy much with it anymore. In desperation, he decided to look for employment with a major seed company in Erfurt, 100 miles away. This particular firm had been my father's major seed supplier for many years, going back to his needs in Estonia.

Rucksack strapped on his back, he said his good-byes before pedaling off on his bicycle. My father's absence heightened the uncertainty that already overwhelmed us. We lived from hour to hour and day to day, not expecting to hear from him for awhile. We scrounged for food and waited. Besides C-rations, strange little comic books were discarded everywhere by the GIs. I made a serious attempt to read these fascinating picture books. But I was completely frustrated. Even after hours of effort, I could understand neither the humor nor the distortions of the pictures nor the language in the balloons of dialogue text.

My father reappeared less than a week after leaving, and not on his bicycle. He wore clothes that were not his own. We all did double takes. His story, as I remember it:

The highway towards Erfurt was completely empty, except for the occasional American military convoy. Kind people put him up the first night and shared their dinner. But on the next day out, he ran into trouble. "Suddenly, when I was just coming around a bend, a group of men jumped out of the woods," he said. "They threw a stick into my wheels—I came down hard." The robbers jumped Father and stripped him of his clothes, his boots, watch, wedding ring, and knapsack—everything except his undershorts. "Just left me almost naked with a smashed bicycle," he said. Before the last man disappeared into the forest, he put on Fathers' boots and tossed his old ones to him.

My father stood for an hour along the roadside, but eventually a truck came by. It was going back in the direction of Salzfurt-kapelle. The driver gave my father an old shirt and took him as far as Halle, dropping him at the apartment of old friends. Luckily, he had memorized Hermann Neumann's address.

Recalling the moment, my father burst out laughing: "You should have seen their faces!" he said. "They almost didn't recognize me. Here I was just in an old shirt, a pair of undershorts, and filthy boots without laces." But they recovered soon and prepared hot water for a long bath. Hermann gave my father some of his own clothes and shoes, and the next day supplied enough money to take a train back to Bobbau. My father walked the last three miles to Salzfurtkapelle in shoes that were too small and made his feet hurt. But he was far more thankful than angry. "I'm lucky to be alive," he said. "Those Russian prisoners could have killed me or broken my bones." My father later admitted that trying that bike trip to Erfurt in the lawless days of immediate post-war Germany was a greater risk than he should have dared to run.

We went back to awaiting developments, subsisting on fresh vegetables, berries, milk from the diary and a protein supply from American rations. The leftovers included powdered eggs, condensed milk and rich Hershey chocolate syrup along with cans of unidentifiable combinations of meat and vegetables. My father found several soldiers who spoke German and became particularly friendly with a German-speaking captain. He contacted two Finnish speakers too, and from them received a steady supply of Lucky Strikes.

The captain was the first to tell my father that the Americans would be vacating our area. An agreement made by President Harry Truman, British Prime Minister Clement Attlee and Josef Stalin at the Cecilianhof Palace in Potsdam at the end of July had set down the final division of Germany. The Western allies would share in a four-power military government set up in Soviet-occupied Berlin. In exchange U.S. and British forces would pull back to a line many miles west of where they had wound up at the end of the war. Salzfurtkapelle fell well within this sector of exchange.

The American captain knew enough of our family's history by now to sympathize with my father's distress at the news. So he offered our family space on an open American truck. Together with American GIs, we would drive the next night for an undisclosed distance to an undisclosed place in the West. The captain couldn't —or wouldn't—tell Father where. We would be allowed to bring nothing except one handbag per person. It meant leaving crates of family paintings and whatever other few valuables Father had salvaged from Majkow. But my parents were determined to leave.

Things then happened very fast. Overnight, I sickened with a very high fever. I have no memory of any family discussions. I started to hallucinate and shook violently. My mother feared that I might have typhoid. Salzfurtkapelle's water was still contaminated. Mother worried that I would die in her arms riding an open truck through the night. She refused to let us leave. That's how we came to stay in Salzfurtkapelle—and how I came to spend my next six years under Soviet and East German communism.

I don't remember when the Soviet troops arrived. Most likely I was still sick—I eventually survived my fever without medicines. Ulf remembers that the first Russian troops came in on horse and wagon a day or so after the Americans left. The soldiers were filthy and their horses seemed starved. Initially, there was no shooting, no shouting, no looting. But we and other refugees were ordered to vacate the manor house within days. A Soviet colonel was to move in and use the house as his headquarters.

On a borrowed bicycle, my father canvassed the neighboring villages for an apartment. The first day he came home without results. But on the second day he brought good news. Herr and Frau Lorenz, the elderly owners of an egg hatchery in Siebenhausen, were willing to give up the second floor of their house. Siebenhausen, not even big enough to have a central square, was of course the same village that Ulf and I had so gleefully watched being shelled.

Chapter 12

The Lorenzes had lost their brood houses, hens and incubators in the shelling of Siebenhausen. Their home itself was still intact, with pockmarks from shrapnel across the front. We Bremens moved into an apartment with a living room and four bedrooms on the second floor, a wonder compared to our one and a half cramped rooms in Salzfurtkapelle. We shared the large country kitchen and coal-burning stove only with our hostess, Frau Lorenz, who was a polio victim and used a walker. Grandmama's joy at regaining a room of her own impressed me so much that I remember her smiles down to this day. I split a bedroom with Fräulein von Voigt, her diary nowhere in sight.

We immediately started a new fall vegetable garden. My father had salvaged only a few green tomatoes and large bag of green beans when forced to abandon our ripening patch at the Osterlands' to the Soviet colonel. All that wonderful fresh food! In exchange for refuge with the Lorenzes, we set to work helping repair the courtyard buildings, tending the potato fields and working the orchards. Within a week, Fräulein von Voigt, Ulf and I were picking the apples and pears. We labored as many as ten or twelve hours a day, but had even less to eat than in Salzfurtkapelle. The approaching winter had brought the realization that Germany, choked with refugees, might be facing starvation. The farmers in Siebenhausen simply locked their doors, refusing to sell milk, eggs or grain, or even to trade for our apples. The year's potato crop wasn't ready. All that I remember is apples and *Weltschmerz* three times a day. How we missed the high-protein American C-rations!

Not having Fräulein Lukas to feed was a blessing. Not having her to tend Grandmama was a curse. The task now fell mainly on my mother. Grandmama's insomnia had returned. She missed the fresh Swiss chard leaves which had helped her so much in Majkow. Sleeping in the room next to her, I heard her talk to herself a lot. Over and over again she repeated her favorite poetry. I heard her recite a Song of Solomon so often that I will never forget it myself.

> My beloved spake and said unto me,
> Rise up, my love, my fair one, and come away.
> For lo, the winter is past,
> The rain is over and gone;
> The flowers appear on the earth;
> The time of the singing of birds is come,
> And the voice of the turtledove is heard in our land;
> The fig tree ripeneth her green figs;
> And the vines are in bloom;
> They give forth their fragrance.
> Arise, my love, my fair one, and come away.

Schools in our region re-opened in the fall of 1945. The closest high school was in Bitterfeld, the chemical center, a half hour rail trip away. But the trains were barely running. My mother searched hard and was fortunate to find room and board for Ulf and me with Frau Krüger, the widow of a Protestant bishop. She lived with her own four children on the third floor of the parsonage, a large townhouse in the center of the city facing the main Lutheran church.

To compensate Frau Krüger, my parents promised a supply of potatoes and apples for the winter. This amazed me. I had no idea where they thought they would find 500 pounds of potatoes. We had none to eat ourselves. Weeks later they told me they hoped to glean enough from the local fields after the harvest to fulfill their promise and to feed us as well.

My memories of these hard post-war months are random snapshots of survival. A common dread of Red Army soldiers, especially among women, hung in the air of Bitterfeld. The women were frightened by their very sight. This is something I had not felt in Siebenhausen, only six miles away, where no Soviet troops were ever stationed. Rape was not discussed with either my mother or Frau Krüger. But, as I later learned, waves of mass rape had swept through many East German cities and towns during the months after the conquest, and Bitterfeld, according to a later history, had experienced an especially "shocking" amount.

Within my first week at Kirchplatz 4, Frau Krüger discovered that I had a lively and growing colony of lice. She must have seen me idly scratching my head. Frau Krüger, a woman of great resource, located a can of kerosene, which she poured on my opened braids, then wrapped my head in a big towel. I don't know what was worse, the smell or the sting on my scalp. Twelve hours later she shampooed it out, but not before sending my mother a scathing letter about the "disgrace" she and her children had suffered. She fretted aloud over it again and again. I began worrying that I was going to be sent home if the kerosene didn't do its duty. After a second kerosene and turban treatment the next day, Frau Krüger pronounced me cured. I felt unbelievable relief. We refugees were foreigners everywhere. I wanted so much to fit in.

The school building, the *Oberschule für Mädchen* (High School for Girls), had served as temporary quarters for Red Army troops. They had broken the toilets and sinks, burned some of the desks and destroyed the heating system. In the science lab, smashed equipment lay about awaiting repair or removal. On one long set of shelves stood rows of heavy, wide-mouthed glass jars with broken tops. These held incredibly shriveled animal and human embryos that had until recently been preserved, life-sized, in alcohol. The soldiers, ignoring the specimens, had drunk the fluid. Or so we were told.

There were no textbooks. All of the Nazi texts, even those for math and science, had been burned by Soviet troops in the court-yard. We could still see the huge blackened patch on the ground. Our teachers, most of them women, taught from scribbled notes that they had apparently taken down themselves not long before, either from lectures by authorities, or their own research, or from memory. The only young male teacher we had was our PE teacher. His face bore witness to unimaginable horrors he had seen, and his right jacket sleeve was empty. Refugees like Ulf and I lacked even writing materials. After several weeks, we were finally given the name of a store that had received a shipment of pads and pencils and were able to buy them.

We sat in our overcoats, hats and mittens as fall turned into winter. I remember the music teacher, who was also the choir direc-tor of our Lutheran church, putting us through breathing and voice lessons. We giggled watching the long whiffs of steam spouting from our fellow students' mouths with each note sung into the cold air.

After school, Ulf and I paid almost daily visits to the big mes-sage board put up in the vestibule of our church. The boards had sprung up everywhere, covered with handwritten notes from refu-gees trying to locate loved ones and friends. Families seeking infor-mation on missing German soldiers posted plaintive notes too. My parents had asked us to look out for news as well as to post mes-sages about friends we had lost contact with. The only response to any of the notes we left was an unsigned piece of paper about Baron and Baroness von Ungern Sternberg, the temporary trek leaders who had initially led us out of Majkow. The writer of the note said that he had heard that the Ungerns had not only survived but had somehow trekked with their own horses all the way to Paris.

My school hours at that time were from eight to twelve noon. After that came the food lines. They haunt me still. Rain, shine or frost, our afternoons were usually spent standing in queues in front

Gate of our farmhouse in Siebenhausen.

of the bakery, the butcher shop, the pharmacy, or the vegetable market. Ration stamps had become meaningless. Stores opened only when they had something to sell. Shopkeepers frequently left a handwritten note on the door, announcing the time a specific product would be available. Sometimes the word came as just a rumor: at nine in the morning a certain store was going to get a shipment of something. Lines immediately formed. You might then wait in a crowd for hours, only to be told through a crack of the door that no, there was no sugar or flour or pork or soap. One never knew if it had all been pure rumor, or if there had been supplies that were sold out the back door to preferred customers, or if shoppers at the front had actually bought something before you were turned aside.

Frau Krüger often joined such lines in the morning. She would leave us a note with instructions to relieve her when we came home from school. We children would then take turns in the line. One unusually cold day in December I found a note to replace Frau Krüger in a queue at the marketplace. A rumor said a farm wagon loaded with cauliflower was coming. Frau Krüger, cold and discouraged, flashed me a wan smile of relief, and I took her place in a crowd of a hundred packed and stomping people. No horse-drawn wagon was yet in sight. Hours passed. It began turning dark. I lost all feeling in my feet, stamping them dumbly and growing steadily more frightened as the numbness climbed above my ankles. My hands were ice blocks too. I'd been cold many times before, but this was different. When the wagon finally came, the crowd surged forward. I'm short in height. I thought for a moment that I was going to be crushed or trampled amid the pushing chests and bellies and feet. But I was fairly well up front, and somehow managed to hold my ground and emerge with one head of cauliflower cradled like a baby in my arms. I then tottered on frozen feet with little baby steps back to the parsonage, where I collapsed in tears. Frau Krüger patiently massaged my whitened toes and hands back to painful life. My feet were not going to fall off! I don't remember eating the cauliflower.

By the second semester of school, life for me had settled down, but not for Ulf. He attended the *Oberschule für Jungen* (High School for Boys) in another part of town. He seemed to have no school chums and was isolated in the Krüger home amid a cloud of females. Frau Krüger presided, and her three daughters and I set the tone, chattering about clothes we did not have and whispering about the sanitary napkins we could not get. Heni, short for

Irene, was the youngest daughter and my best friend. We were the same age, shared the same school class and the same unheated room in the mansard under the roof of the parsonage. I learned the wonders of a German featherbed up there. Mine was not only warm and cozy in the freezing air, but a spiritual comfort through many nights of worry and uncertainty about my teenage future.

We absorbed Frau Krüger's frustration with the new political system that was evolving in the *Sovietische Besatzungs Zone* (Soviet Occupation Zone). Large red street banners had gone up in Bitterfeld celebrating Rosa Luxemburg and Karl Liebknecht, the heroic German communist leaders murdered in 1919 after the unsuccessful Spartacist Uprising in Berlin. Other banners saluted Karl Marx and, of course, Lenin. By the second term, a formal "Anti-fascist Democratic School Reform" program had been launched. We now got a little political indoctrination in all the classes, and a straight dose of reeducation during our class on current events. The teacher of this session still had no formal textbooks. She worked from mimeographs and her own handwritten notes. But the presentation was systematic. We were learning an entirely new world view, in conflict with everything we had been taught under the Nazis. It might have sunk in more if we had had a textbook to read that made sense of the transformation. Our mandatory first foreign language was now Russian. Second was still Latin and English was third.

When we girls got home, Frau Krüger offered a decisively different political view. A deeply religious woman whose bishop husband had suddenly died of a heart attack, she openly criticized the anti-church leadership that was developing in Bitterfeld. She fueled her anti-communism—perhaps a little unfairly, I think now—by criticizing the long bread lines, the lack of coal and the lack of almost everything in the stores. "Only yesterday," I can still hear her say, "we were asked to follow one dictator, and now we are being asked to follow another with a different set of principles."

Ulf and I took a train home to Bobbau every Saturday afternoon after school. It was a weekly nightmare. The Bitterfeld station had not been damaged in the war. Its large waiting room was heated and invariably attracted big numbers of Russian soldiers. The stench of their filthy uniforms and unwashed bodies and cigarette smoke was unbelievable. (From history books much later I learned that most Soviet troops at that time had often been issued only one uniform.) The soldiers congregated around a steaming bar, drinking tea, beer and schnapps. The trains often ran hours late, but you never knew. I had nothing to do but study the soldiers and ignore their glances. The difference between these conquerors and the rich Americans to my eyes could not have been bigger. The Russians had shaven heads. Their padded olive-green jackets were smeared with dirt. Soviet red stars gleamed from grease-spiked fake fur hats with dangling ear flaps. All this contrasted sharply with the trim military caps and the shiny brass badges on the heads, shoulders and clean collars of the Americans.

The soldiers in the station seemed never to be sober. "*Komm, komm. Frau komm!*" (Come, come. Woman, come!) were the only German words most seemed to have learned. We girls were warned that besides women, the Russian soldiers were keen on watches, and that many had syphilis. I did not know what this meant, but had the vague impression it had something to do with being raped.

When the train to Bobbau finally arrived, Ulf and I became part of a pushing, shoving crowd fighting to get in. Then, after a packed hour-long ride in an unheated car, it became equally hard to get off. Nobody could let us pass without actually stepping off the train themselves. And they were opposed by more people on Bobbau's platform pushing to get in. Darkness had usually fallen when we did struggle off the train. We then had two miles to walk to Siebenhausen through blustery winter weather on an exposed road. I was invariably haunted by my old fears of the dark. Hostile monsters, ghosts and now Russian soldiers seemed to be lurking everywhere. Even Ulf's presence was no help. I have never understood the origin of my fear of darkness; perhaps too many scary stories were told to me in my early childhood by Tatchen in Estonia.

The journey back to Bitterfeld had to be repeated less than a day later, on Sunday afternoon. I don't know why my parents put us through this weekly ordeal for less than a single day at home. It may have been to save Frau Krüger's food supplies. Hunger reigned in Siebenhausen too, but there always seemed to be just a bit more to eat.

We girls at school all looked forward to our first post-war Christmas vacation. At least, we told each other, we would be in a warm house—we could not imagine our families forgoing heat on such a holiday. On Christmas Eve our family in Siebenhausen gathered around a little Christmas tree decorated with ornaments that we ourselves had made. The tinsel came from the aluminum chaff which was dropped by Allied bombers and still littered the cities and countryside. (The bombers had released clouds of these thin, long strips of aluminum, called "chaff," to blind the German anti-aircraft radar that was attempting to fix their location and height.) We cast our own paraffin candles, pouring the heated wax into empty American 20mm brass cannon casings for molds. Piles of such shell casings were all that was left from the fighting in the spring. We cut and stitched pale yellow straw into stars, which we hung among the tinsel and candles on the tree. Polished little red apples from the Lorenzes' orchards completed the decorations. We looked at the result with great admiration, the candlelight glittering on the tinsel and the cheeks of the apples. My mother read St. John's version of the Christmas story. After a cold dinner of potato salad and apple sauce, she started on the first chapter of *Gone with the Wind*. The used book was a Christmas present from Herr and Frau Lorenz. We marveled at the similarity between Scarlett O'Hara's story and our own.

Next spring, my father was asked to work as a Russian translator at a nearby dairy farm. It was going to become a state-owned
collective. Instead of cash payment, my father bartered for a pregnant sheep and two goats. When the animals arrived, Grandmama
was given her first real job since our arrival. She guarded the goats
and sheep as they foraged on grassy patches alongside country
roads. Rain or shine, Grandmama was there playing shepherdess.
She looked unrecognizable to me in a set of face-engulfing sun-
glasses, ankle-length cloak and visored sun hat.

As time went on, my father assumed much of the management of the orchards and vegetable garden from our elderly and
handicapped hosts. Lacking spare parts, he and the Lorenzes were
never able to repair the incubators and chicken houses. But for the
expanding vegetable garden and potato fields, my parents needed
more help. Father's initial efforts to hire the right person were not
successful. It was my mother who found Mina, a refugee like us.
Mina, mentally retarded and of an undetermined age, had found
shelter with her equally destitute sister in a small apartment adjacent to one of the farms in Siebenhausen. The sister had no thumbs,

Grandmama shepherds our goats and pregnant sheep.

only five fingers. A year or so later, I overheard the sisters' landlord say, "I always wondered how they avoided euthanasia in Hitler's concentration camps. But here they are, making the best of the situation."

My mother loved the childish, smiling and toothless Mina. Mother was fascinated by her peculiar habits and strange speech. Her sentences contained words from different languages and many grunts. I could never understand what she was saying, but my mother had the patience to figure it out. Some time after Mina was hired, my mother discovered her wearing a pouch between her legs, covered by her long skirt. Whenever Mina thought that nobody was looking, she stashed away a carrot or other vegetable or fruit. My mother kept this to herself, touched by Mina's determination to survive. Long after my mother had died, I found among her few belongings a pencil sketch of Mina that she had lovingly drawn in profile. The paper had yellowed and the image had faded with time, but Mina's valiant personality comes through in the set of her brow, her mouth, her jaw.

Fräulein von Voigt (left), Mina (middle) and Mother with our goats.

The physical work in the garden and fields that spring made my father and Fräulein von Voigt desperate for protein. She became expert in catching mice. One Sunday morning, home for the weekend, I was startled to see her frying two little carcasses in cod-liver oil, the only oil available to us at that time. Even today, I can still smell that awful fish oil and hear the sound of crunching bones. About the same time, my father discovered a fiber-rich "breakfast cereal" manufactured in the Agfa film factories in nearby Wolfen. The flakes were available for sale everywhere and became quite popular. We all ate them, but my father, thrilled as always with a new technology, ate bowlfuls, and three times a day. Soon, he fell violently ill with food or chemical poisoning. Mother, visiting him in the hospital, was told by his doctor that Father almost died in the first days after his admission. The "breakfast cereal" in question, the doctor said, was made from a petroleum base and was toxic in large amounts. When I first saw my father after his release from the hospital, I thought he looked like Grandmama—just skin and bones and about the same age. He very slowly regained his health.

To a passerby that spring, the scene at Siebenhausen must at times have looked pastoral: Grandmama shepherding the sheep and goats, father in the garden, and mother, Mina and Fräulein von Voigt sitting in the sun outside the kitchen door cleaning vegetables while chicken scurried around their feet. But a closer look would have revealed that we were all badly undernourished and barely getting by.

One Sunday morning in June, when we had just started summer school vacation, I found my mother sitting alone in the kitchen. She appeared agitated, her hands shaking and her face flushed.

"I found this note from Ulf." She pointed to a piece of paper. "He's left to catch the first train out. And he said not to try to stop him. He's leaving and will not return."

My mother slumped over, burying her head in her arms. My

brother, gone? I ran to tell my father, but he was still in bed and I did not dare to wake him. Why would Ulf do such a thing? Why? Not having an immediate answer, I did not worry for too long. I lived then so entirely in my own teenage bubble that I somehow didn't really care too much about Ulf. I was, however, annoyed by the many secret discussions between my parents that followed behind closed doors. Yet there it was. Ulf was gone.

Years later, when I asked my mother about it, she said this: "I could have taken my bike and followed him to the station in time, but I didn't do that. I was terrified to have a confrontation. I knew that I couldn't stop him from leaving."

"When I told Oma," my mother added, "she said that she had found Ulf always *désoeuvré* and destructive. Most likely I had brought it on myself."

My parents left the East German police out of it too. Mother was sure that Ulf would try to cross the border to the western occupation zones. She wrote letters to friends in the West asking them to notify the West German police that he was presumed to be trying to find a job there. She asked to be notified when Ulf was registered, as the law required, at his new place of work.

More than a year passed before my parents got word. My mother received a letter from a police station in Wolfsburg. It said that a single male, Ulf von Bremen, had started work in the Volkswagen automobile factories in Wolfsburg. My mother immediately packed a small suitcase, took a train to Magdeburg and somewhere nearby succeeded in crossing the then-still-lightly-guarded border to the West. She arrived at the auto workers' barracks in Wolfsburg and waited two hours in his room for his shift to end. When he walked in, he was shocked and furious at having been tracked down. He asked her to leave. In desperation, Mother begged him to forgive her for whatever she had done wrong to create the rift in their relationship. Ulf, feeling cornered, screamed at her: "Leave me alone. I don't ever want to see you again." He threw her out.

Three years later, Ulf immigrated to Canada. In the late 1960s, he finally agreed to a visit from my mother. They had been in touch intermittently through letters. In the interim, I learned that Ulf and Father had been at odds for years, both in the Warthegau and in Germany. It had been mostly about his troubles in school and his "lack of growing up," as my father put it. Mother also said that Ulf had failed his classes the year he left Siebenhausen and was being asked to repeat the same grade. When Ulf and I finally resumed a correspondence decades later, I asked him why he had left. His terse answer seems logical and matter-of-fact:

> In a nutshell, I wanted to get away from it all. From my family because they were stagnating and frozen in the past. From Siebenhausen because I could not see myself working full time for one of the farmers, like I did one summer. From the Krüger family in Bitterfeld because they had no food and I depended on their son's hand-me-down clothing. From high school because I was not interested in Pythagoras or *The Walk to Canossa*.

My mother sank more often into the darkness of her depressions following Ulf's flight. She sometimes just sat staring idly into space when I was home. I was uncomfortable seeing her like that, but at the same time, I was afraid to asked questions or comfort her with my support. I was centered on myself, and really only cared about my friends and life in school.

In the winter of 1946, Frau Krüger sickened with worry about the shrinking supply of soft coal in her basement. She heated only the stove in the kitchen as it was. I remember being cold, cold, cold and having colds all the time. Still, each Friday night, she prepared a laundry tub with hot water for us to take a bath. We all shared the same bath water. Frau Krüger always took the last turn. "If we don't wash ourselves at least once a week," she repeatedly explained, "we'll get those dreadful things again." She still couldn't bring herself to use the word "lice."

Eventually, we came to the bottom of the coal pile. Bitterfeld was surrounded by soft coal mines. Frau Krüger knew that many people, even friends, had started to help themselves to coal from the open gondola cars in the rail yard. As a devout Christian, Frau Krüger said that she understood their actions but that theft still was never right.

Finally, one night over dinner she announced that we ourselves would visit the rail yard. She at first called it "an errand." She added that "the Ten Commandments say: 'Thou shall not steal.' But, I'm sure that under the circumstances, God will forgive me for what I'm about to do."

Around midnight, we dragged our sleds with some gunny sacks to the rail yards. The tracks teemed with scores of moving shadows, some scooping coal into bags, others piling it into baby carriages, garden carts and onto sleds. Suddenly, a whistle sounded and armed security guards loomed out of the darkness into the yard lights. Everybody scrambled. We made it home with three bags of coal, which would last us for less than three weeks, even if only used in the kitchen. Days later, Frau Krüger was still saying to us: "I have prayed that God will forgive us for what we have done." I was just happy to have some heat.

In the spring of 1947, when Heni and I were preparing for confirmation to the Lutheran faith, the Eighth Commandment reared its head again. I was home for the weekend when Grandmama accused me of stealing plum jam from her rationed portion in a small glass jar.

"Last night the jar was full," she said. "This morning most of it is gone. You are the only one to have the impudence to take my food."

My shock and hurt gave way to disbelief, and disbelief to anger. I vehemently protested. Grandmama must have become so blind that she was unable to see what she herself had eaten. Grandmama ignored me.

"I will forgive you for it, but only if you confess," she said. "If you don't, I will not give you a present for your confirmation. I was planning on that bracelet with diamonds."

I surely wanted that bracelet—Grandmama had wonderful jewelry. But I was not prepared to confess to a crime I did not commit.

Confirmation into the faith of my parents took place in the Lutheran church on the Kirchplatz. Heni and I wore severe little black dresses, our thick braids tied with white ribbons. My parents, only casually religious themselves, came to the ceremony. Fräulein von Voigt and Grandmama did not. After the church service, we gathered for a festive meal. My parents had brought a chicken, which Frau Krüger had promised to roast.

I loved all the hens we had in Siebenhausen. But the one Mother selected for the dinner was my absolute favorite. That little hen reminded me of my beloved Babette in Solitude. To chop off the hen's head, she used the same hatchet and wood block we used to split firewood. I almost became sick as I saw the blood squirt out

My confirmation in Bitterfeld: front row, 3rd from left; me; 5th from left: Heni Krüger. Back row, 3rd from left: Mother; 5th from left: Father. Between them Bishop Fritsche.

of the neck when the hatchet came down. I could hardly eat anything at the celebration. Grandmama stuck to her word. I got no present, let alone the bracelet with diamonds.

Inadvertently, Grandmama did save me from being raped. One night when I was home from school in the fall of 1947, everyone was asleep except my father and Fräulein von Voigt. They had stayed up to finish cooking a batch of molasses from sugar beets. The lights of the kitchen apparently attracted the attention of Soviet soldiers driving past on the Autobahn. My father knew nothing until he heard banging on the locked gate. Before he could check on the noise, the soldiers had broken down the gate and driven their truck into the courtyard. Instantly, the group posted a guard on my father and Fräulein von Voigt in the kitchen while others fanned out into the house. They came to the sleeping Lorenzes first, surprising them with demands for watches, clocks and jewelry.

"The soldiers were drunk," said Frau Lorenz. "They ripped off my rings and took my husband's gold watch. But when they saw my crippled legs, they left our room in a hurry."

I was asleep on a sofa in our living room upstairs and woke up with the uneasy feeling of somebody looking at me. When I opened my eyes, I peered into the barrel of a machine gun and then into the eyes of a Soviet soldier. He looked at me with undisguised lust. Paralyzed with fear, I could not scream. I was certain about what was going to happen next. But where were my parents? Why were they not here to protect me? He took off his coat and put down his gun. Just then, another soldier rushed into the room, shouting something I could not understand. My soldier grabbed his coat and gun and they were both gone in seconds, running down the stairs. Soon I heard the truck's engine roaring in the effort to back out of the courtyard and leave.

I rushed at the door of my parents' bedroom. My mother had locked herself in. How could she do this? I was furious.

"I was mostly worried about myself," my mother said, unlocking her door. "I listened from the other side and would have come out. But I didn't think that you were in any danger. You're just a child."

The betrayal, the anger I felt then is indescribable. I was not saved by her, my own mother!

It turned out, in fact, that Grandmama had driven them away.

"I heard the commotion," she told us. "From their voices I knew that they were Russian peasants and that they were drunk. If they are peasants, I thought, then they will be afraid of ghosts. There was only one thing for me to do."

At her age it was not hard to accomplish. She lit a single candle on her nightstand. She ruffled her white hair into a wild halo. She threw off her covers, leaving her near-skeleton of 90 pounds draped only in her white gown. She sat up in bed and propped her cane between her legs, her hands folded high up on the handle. She then began rocking back and forth, muttering loudly to herself.

"When the door opened, my candle flickered in the draft, throwing ghostly shadows on the wall," Grandmama said with a chuckle. "I think that if I could have seen myself, I would have been scared of my own image too. I saw him come in. He took one look at me and let out a terrible oath. Then he was gone."

That soldier was the one who burst in and spooked my would-be rapist.

"I was afraid they would steal my jewelry," said Grandmama. "Ah well," she added with a thin smile, "they were nothing but half-witted peasant boys."

Maybe so. My scare was nothing measured against the slaughters, tortures and rapes endured by millions of people during and after the war. But no woman who has looked into the eyes of a rapist will ever forget her fright.

Chapter 13

The three post-war years blend in my memory into equal parts hunger, cold, scarcity, school, and a shared sense of making do under grim circumstances. Even our sweets were sour. There was never enough sugar to remove the bitterness from the elderberries and currants that we canned, or to lift our raspberry or strawberry jams out of neutrality. I haven't tried elderberry jelly again to this day. I cannot contemplate a jar of the stuff without a pucker wrinkling my lips. We ate so many beets that it took me half a century before I was willing to sample again this delicious root. I'm sure there must have been some light, some laughter during these years, but if there was, my mind refuses to recall it.

The year 1948 brought change. Spring came warm and early and with it my first real feelings of optimism and hope. The last months of my schooling were flashing by. The Lorenz farm seemed ever more prosperous when I visited each weekend. Together with the clouds of white and pink apple blossoms in the orchard, there was my father lovingly tending masses of tomato seedlings in a cold frame. Gardening lifted his and the whole family's mood. A goat gave birth again, this time with twins. Thanks to the small flock of chickens, we now sometimes had fresh eggs for breakfast. I shed my patched winter clothes and one more time let out the seams and hems of the few dresses I owned. We all had more to eat. Mother's friends, those in her Zwingenberg Group living in the West, came through again. They were prospering enough to send heavenly packages stuffed with sugar, milk and egg powder, oatmeal, Spam, and occasional real coffee.

At school I do recall one shocker, a denunciation. Through out my few years there, I remember a teacher only once asking us for names of family members or others who were Nazis or were speaking against the new government. When this request did come, it sounded familiar. Not that long before, a teacher in Kalisz had routinely asked us to report any anti-government conversations we might have heard at home. No one had ever arisen, at least not in public. Now, I was stunned when a girl stood up and declared:

"My parents are an enemy of the people and to communism. They both were Nazis. I apologize to the authorities for not having reported this earlier." Our political instruction by this time was part of the daily routine. But I still could not imagine how she could do this to her own father and mother.

Then something else happened. Our current events teacher announced one morning that the whole school would go to the country the next day to pick beetles from young potato plants. The insects were destroying the fields. It was our duty as young communists, the teacher said, to support the country during this economic crisis. We had each to bring a cup from home, which we'd fill and then dump into covered buckets. The student who collected the most beetles was promised a certificate signed by Erich Honecker, founder of the *Freie Deutsche Jugend* (Free German Youth, the East German communist youth organization). With a straight face, the teacher said that the American capitalists were trying to sabotage socialism by dropping these yellow-and-black-striped beetles on us from the air. I can't remember if I really believed this. We were fed so much anti-Western information that some of it got swallowed.

We picked beetles from plants in the vast potato fields for two days. Our teachers sat at the side of the road, gossiping. I can't remember how many cups I picked, but certainly not enough to receive a written citation. I was far too busy filling my pockets and underwear with tiny baby potatoes I took when nobody was look-

ing. I had learned something from Mina, even if I lacked a pouch
between my legs. Frau Krüger was delighted with the windfall, and
never asked the details of how I got them.

I couldn't wait to complete my *Mittlere Reife* (Middle Level,
equivalent to a high school degree). I was sick of school and wanted
out. I thought that I had worked hard that last year, but I was still a
C student. My final report card gave proof—the only Bs I received
were in geography, art and physical education. No A's. My problem
was, I really did not care. The teachers' remarks noted: "Sigrid tried
to improve her grades to become a better student. She leaves school
to start a career in dress design."

Frau Krüger and her daughters violently opposed this decision. We argued about it for weeks. I suffered my first rift with
Heni, who would stay two more years for her *Abitur* (the college
preparatory degree), and then go on to a university. She looked at
me now a little as if I were a stranger. The subject never came up
with my parents. Women in my mother's and grandmother's class
and generation in Estonia usually went to finishing school, not university. Grandmama and my mother graduated from Finn, the
most prestigious school for young women in the country. In the
Soviet Zone in 1948, an education of this kind was not to be imagined. My parents, farming from dawn to dusk, must mainly have
been happy that I was not going to leave them like Ulf. We refugees were not really rooted anywhere. My apprenticeship as a dressmaker would at least be in Bitterfeld.

Nearing graduation, I wrote my mother a classic letter from a
teenager anticipating her first big dance:

...We're having our final prom in 14 days...I think it all
will be quite nice. Included in the evening events will be
dances and theatre performances. Dear Mutti, may I cut my
hair for this? Please, please say yes. But don't say anything to
Paps, he most certainly would not allow it. Tomorrow I have

my Latin final. Keep your fingers crossed for me. I'm not sure I'll be able to sleep. I kiss you good night.

My mother must have given permission, because in a prom picture, I am in short hair wearing a long dress. To my great distress and embarrassment, my escort showed up with only paper flowers. Most of my classmates, at least those who mattered, received real ones. My first reaction was to casually leave mine behind. Then I decided to keep them for the polonaise and make the best of it. I don't remember much about the prom, except for the kiss on the way home. It was my first and it was wet and wonderful.

My optimism crashed just days after graduation. I came down with a painful staph infection of the glands under my arms and in my crotch. I went to Siebenhausen to heal. The throbbing carbuncles kept me in bed and awake all night. Lancing them hurt more than it helped. My lovely mother tried to comfort me, but she was strangely remote and indifferent. I saw her several times a day all that summer and early fall. But I was too young to see that her depressions were evolving towards a breakdown.

The infection finally cleared and I entered training in October with Frau Louise Döhner, one of the biggest names in dressmaking in Bitterfeld. Born and educated in Paris, she, her husband and unmarried daughter lived and worked on the ground floor of a spacious apartment. That first day Frau Döhner warned me that I could be fired if I ever pricked my finger while handling fabrics. Even good curtain materials at that time were incredibly dear, and blood stains on fabrics were impossible to remove. My fellow seamstresses that same day issued a second warning: Herr Döhner was a menace. He slept during the day and spent nights carousing in town.

I heard him come home in the morning a few weeks later when we were already at work. He belched and cursed while banging his way to the master bedroom in the rear. A few minutes later, he reappeared in the workroom, wearing nothing but a bulging belly.

"I'll catch one of you girls." He slurred his words, blocking the door to the outside. "Which one of you wants to come and snuggle with me?"

Frau Döhner jumped from her stool and threw open a window. "Quick," she said. "Jump and be gone."

She remained behind as we stunned girls jumped. We scampered down the block, stopped, stared back down the empty street, sat on the curb, giggling nervously, and waited. Eventually Frau Döhner returned us to our sewing machines, assuring us that Herr Döhner was now asleep in his bed. No explanation! No apology! We whispered what a terrible man he was and how sorry we felt for his wife.

Academic classes for apprentice dressmakers convened every Thursday. We studied the history of natural dyes and fabrics, how to make dress and coat patterns to our own measurements, a dozen other technical matters. In current events, we learned again of the evils of Hitler's tyranny, then moved to the glorious hope of the first two-year economic plan developed for us by the new SED, the *Sozialistische Einheits Partei Deutschlands* (Socialist Unity Party of Germany). This was the name assumed by the German communist party when it took over the Soviet Zone and founded the German Democratic Republic (*Deutsche Demokratische Republik*, the DDR) in 1949. Our final grades in current events, the teacher warned, would count more towards our dressmaker's diploma than would our technical studies. I remember writing dutiful and glowing political essays, one about our great new DDR government and another about its first president, Wilhelm Pieck, who had spent decades in exile in the Soviet Union.

I still visited my parents at home on the odd weekend. One Saturday we had finished dinner and were about to have dessert, the first ripe melon from the garden. We sat at the kitchen table in our usual seats: Mother at the head, Grandmama to her right and I to her left. My father and Fräulein von Voigt were across from each other further down. They were deeply involved in their own conversation, unaware of anybody else in the room. Suddenly, my mother rose from her chair, grabbed the melon, lifted it high over her head and slammed it down. Chips of broken plates mixed with pink melon pulp flew everywhere. My mother had pushed back her chair with such force that it had crashed to the floor. We sat frozen in our seats as she rushed out of the room. I heard her stumble on the stairs, but she did not fall. My father, his face in a grimace, rushed out after her.

I tiptoed into her room the next day to say goodbye before going back to Bitterfeld. "I just want to go to sleep and not wake up," she said quietly, and then said it again. I didn't know how to respond. I finally tiptoed out. For days afterward my mother stayed in bed, refusing food and sympathy, keeping her shades down and wanting no visitors. Back in Bitterfeld, I spent sleepless nights myself, worrying about what had brought on Mother's breakdown and what would happen next. Mother had suffered earlier attacks of despair, but nothing like this. Was it, finally, my father's relationship with

Fräulein von Voigt? Was it Grandmama? Was it Ulf's absence? Was it me? Was it the hopelessness of our future? Maybe it was all of these together. I mentioned my mother's breakdown to no one. Mental illness in that era brought shame to victim and family. Secrecy prevailed. It took many weeks, but slowly, my mother brought herself

Fräulein von Voigt working in the potato patch.

back from the edge. One weekend I arrived to find her on her feet, going about the daily routines but smiling hardly at all. Decades later, when she came on a visit to New York City, I asked her if the melon incident had anything to do with Fräulein von Voigt and my father.

"Those were horrible days," she said. "I barely survived them. I rather wanted to die than go on. Helene von Voigt was certainly one of the problems, but so was Grandmama, and the terrible uncertainty about Ulf." Then she added, brightly, "But now that I am corresponding with Ulf, and Helene von Voigt is gone, and Grandmama is dead, I have found peace with Paps."

I probed for more.

"I was at the end of my rope. I had lost all support from Paps. He and Fräulein von Voigt made all the decisions, as if I didn't exist. Grandmama accused me of being too weak to fire her. She would say, 'Just get rid of her.' As if I had a choice. We needed her work in the garden so that we had a place with the Lorenzes and something to eat. And every day Grandmama herself attacked me. It was either the way I had brought up my children or that I did not pay enough attention to her. Eventually I put it to Paps to decide: Either both Grandmama and Fräulein von Voigt will go, or I will go myself."

Months passed after Mother's breakdown before she actually delivered that ultimatum. Meanwhile, I returned to my routine at Frau Döhner's. I liked everything about dresses. We converted curtains, bedspreads and even the occasional shawl into dresses and skirts for women desperate for anything to wear. But Frau Döhner's best and most profitable clients came from the new elite, the wives of black marketers. These women brought their own fabrics, beautiful stuff obviously smuggled in from the West. When they came for their fittings, we seamstresses took turns peeking through a key hole to catch a glimpse of these fashionable women. They were young, some not much older than I, and in most cases connected to older men, older even than my father. But I still admired them for their clothes and secretly hoped that some day I could look just like they did. Over time, wives of factory bigwigs and various SED big shots became our clients too. But they were usually no match in glamour to our first clientele.

On my own time, I made a skirt and blouse from a curtain my mother had traded for garden produce. Instead of going home most weekends, I went out dancing in my fine new clothes with a friend. I had met Sonja in high school. Now Sonja, a dental technician, introduced me to boys and jazz. We listened many evenings to American jazz and broadcasts from RIAS (Radio in the American Sector) in her living room. RIAS was one of several western radio stations forbidden to us in the DDR. We turned off the lights, hoping that this way nobody could see us sitting in front of the radio. Sonja's father shocked us by calling us stupid about the lights. He said the *Stasi (Staats Sicherheits Dienst,* the State Security Service) agents had listening devices that could hear anything inside a house from quite a distance away.

The dance halls on Saturday nights charged for entry at the door, but offered live music by big bands. Young guys my age would ask for a dance, and if things worked out, they might pay for a glass of beer. It was all quite innocent. But both Frau Krüger and her daughters strongly disapproved. How horribly staunch were these Krügers in their faith and culture! Frau Krüger even threatened to write to my mother explaining exactly why I didn't come home more often on weekends. I don't know if she did. My mother never mentioned it. Mother, after all, had terrible problems of her own.

She finally gained the strength and courage to give my father her ultimatum in the summer of 1950. Either Grandmama and Fräulein von Voigt would leave the house or she would go, forever. Fräulein von Voigt could find another job, she said. Grandmama, now 88, could go to a retirement home. Mother also insisted that she and Father move to another apartment where they could start a new life. Behind her demands, I suddenly realized with a shock, was a determination not only to hold on to her own life, but to hold on to her marriage. She knew my father's heart. Even Grandmama had to go. Perhaps especially Grandmama had to go. What an awful burden she had been, and for thirty years. I found a bitter letter penned by Grandmama, dated October 1948, when she was still sharing my parents' house, in my father's desk after he died. I find it fascinating that it was kept and not destroyed. She wrote:

> My dear children,
>
> Before complete darkness settles on my eyes, while I can still write, I would like to tell you what is on my mind.
>
> I want to thank you for letting me live under your roof, letting me eat at your table, and for all your help and gifts. All of this, of course, I expected, after giving you all that remained of my inherited estate.
>
> I want to forgive you your indifferences and your neglect, which have sorely hurt me. I also forgive my grandchildren for their untruthfulness and rudeness. They were encouraged in these habits by you when you failed to reprimand them. Indulgent love comes at a great cost to the children. God sent you repeated warnings—Bill's illness, Ulf's accident, Sigrid's infection—and I ask God that he may not remove from you his blessings.
>
> I am indeed willful and irritable, but I've always stood fast alongside you. I could have been driven from the house, but God has prevented it. And now, when I am going blind, I find hardly any empathy for my frailty. I've even been accused of faking.
>
> I also forgive Fräulein von Voigt her unbecoming insolence…

Grandmama, in this extraordinary outpouring of her frustrations, concludes by evoking her adoptive son Sten as a rebuke to my father. Sten had returned to his natural parents in Sweden back in 1914 but had remained in touch by letter. "Sten," she wrote, "has been more loving and understanding than my own natural son."

Two years after Grandmama wrote this message, my father heard and agreed to Mother's demands. My parents announced that Fräulein von Voigt was leaving. She had found another job as caretaker of a distant relative, an invalid who was living by himself. I lost track of her for several decades, but my father stayed in touch through letters, and even a rare visit. She later wrote that she was "devastated by the separation" and her life thereafter seems to have been incredibly lonely. She cared for one invalid after another, for low wages and her keep. She had four sisters. But not once did she talk of them in my presence and never did she mention them in letters that she wrote to me.

She seems to have lived partly in constant reverie over her ten years with my father and our family. An incredible stream-of-consciousness letter to me at Father's death spoke of nothing in her life but us. She evoked incident after long-forgotten incident from Majkow and Siebenhausen, and expressed her joy at Father's later sharing of the details of my parents' subsequent lives and vacation travels. She even expressed delight for my father that he had found companionship and love in a brief second marriage before he died. She described in detail the postcard Father sent her from his honeymoon in Lanzarote. This from a woman who might have expected that the second wife should have been her!

Despite the misery she brought to my mother, I cannot help but be touched by her unleashed passion, and the loneliness that must often have been her life. "I will be forever grateful," she wrote, conveying in a sentiment repeated several times, "to have been privileged to know your family and your incomparable father …Now this house is closed for me forever."

Shortly after Helene von Voigt departed, Grandmama moved to the *Alba Langenskold Heim,* a home in the western sector of Berlin for Baltic German aristocrats in their old age. A wealthy Swede had endowed it. Although Grandmama intermittently complained, her first letter to my parents was ecstatic. "I'm surrounded by people I know and who care about me. It's almost like being back in Estonia." To finance her stay, Grandmama had agreed to sell her jewelry. But as my mother found out, we were not the only people desperate for cash. Hundreds of strapped Berliners and refugees were selling their family jewels and table silver. The glut drove down the price. My mother got only about half the sum she'd hoped for. Included in the sale, of course, was the famous bracelet with diamonds. At this point I had lost all interest in owning such a treasure.

With Grandmama now out of the way, my parents moved to a second floor apartment in a modern building on Alte Strasse in Bobbau, a small town two miles away. I loved visiting these new quarters. For the first time in years, we had our own kitchen and a bathroom with indoor plumbing. In Siebenhausen we'd had a single fresh water tap in the shared kitchen, and no access to the Lorenz bathroom on the first floor. We all, including Grandmama, had used the outdoor privy.

Father started a new garden, by my count his sixth, in three different countries. Along with the new garden plot came a small arbor. I remember him sitting happily under its vines, wearing shorts and occasionally lighting up one of his favorite Russian *papyrosies*.

A few months later, on January 1, 1951, he took a new job—a good one, but with an ancient enemy. My father spoke four languages fluently and was hired as the personal interpreter to the Soviet military director of the Agfa Film and Dye Factories in nearby Wolfen. For my father it must have been something of a humiliation to depend for work on the nation and ideology that had engineered his downfall. But the DDR was starting to force even small East German farms into state-owned collectives. Apolitical as he was, he risked being reduced to a collective farm worker if he remained in agriculture. So city work beckoned. The official process of de-Nazification and political clearance went quickly. Father had never been a Party member, and the Russians ignored or did not explore his pre-revolutionary class status and post-revolutionary actions. The director, a Soviet general, was desperate for a linguist.

The shipment of finished products from East German factories to Russia, and even portions of the factories themselves, was part of Stalin's post-war claim for reparations. In the case of Agfa, the Soviet state took direct ownership and shipped both products and machinery east. My father never could grasp why the Soviets never sent Agfa engineers along with the complex machinery to reinstall it. Rumors had it that the loaded railroad cars eventually came to rest on some distant Polish or Soviet rail siding, where the machines simply rusted away. The engineers in Wolfen, in the meantime, improvised continuing production at the factories as best they could.

My father had a cordial relationship with his new boss, a much-decorated officer and staunch Communist Party member. They got along well because neither asked the other any questions about his past. The Soviet secret police, the KGB, on the other hand, kept track of my father almost around the clock.

My father (seated, right) at Agfa company party.

To the delight of his co-workers, my father started a window box garden. Pink begonias with white petunias mixed in were soon in constant bloom. But even these paled in comparison to the scarlet fire bean vine. By the time full summer arrived, the vine, festooned with Soviet-red blossoms, had reached the top of the window frame and then marched forward along the curtain rod.

Father himself soon gained as much fame as this vine. On the first day of full summer heat, he arose in the apartment in Bobbau, donned a pair of Bermuda shorts and an open-necked polo shirt, and biked as usual to his office in Wolfen. Short pants were unheard of in Eastern Europe as business clothes, let alone in the West. They struck a glaring contrast to the boxy Soviet suits and uniforms that clothed the general. Everyone in the factory soon made some excuse to drift by and take a look at this strange Jack and his beanstalk.

It did not take long before my father received a hand-written note saying that the shorts were not compatible with the importance of his job. The note also said that the fire bean vine was unacceptable too. Both had to go.

The truth is that my father had always hated suits, hated any kind of business or formal wear. Only on occasions such as weddings, funerals and later board meetings with top Soviet communists at the factory would he grudgingly submit to wearing a tie. I found only one gray suit and three wrinkled ties among his belongings after he died.

My father stuffed the general's note in his pocket and returned the next day wearing his Bermuda shorts. He also continued to welcome anyone who came to admire the flaming red flowers on his vine. More days passed. Then he received another note, this time on factory stationery. He was fired.

I found my father puttering in his garden when I came home the next weekend after. My mother told me about Paps' discharge and what had happened since. She had instantly worried that the Russians might punish him. And if they didn't, where could Paps find another job, having been fired by our victors? More days passed. My father, seemingly unconcerned, spent most of his time staking his tomato plants. Then came a knock at the door. My mother opened it and was startled to find a stern-faced Soviet soldier. He handed her a sealed envelope. Inside was a note handwritten on plain white paper, signed by father's former boss. The Agfa director wanted him to return to work and "could he come right away?" My father changed from his garden shorts into his office Bermudas, put on a clean shirt and followed the soldier into the black limo parked outside.

I asked Father what had happened when he got to the office. "The director looked at me and said, 'Herr Bremen, you are still not wearing proper business attire.' I said, 'Comrade General, shorts are what I wear in the summer.' He shrugged, handed me some documents, and said, 'Please get these translated by tonight.' He hasn't mentioned the shorts since."

Everything thereafter at Agfa remained the same. The surveillance continued, my father wore his shorts, and the bean vine pushed out many, many more fiery blossoms.

I finished my apprenticeship with Frau Döhner in 1951. My final "exam" was to create a fancy dress from scratch. I made my sketch, cut my own patterns and bought the only fabric I could get, a yellow material that was 100% synthetic. It was limp, difficult to work with, and easily stretched out of shape. Despite all that, I felt that I had completed a masterpiece when finished. Proudly, I wore it a few times dancing with Sonja.

Two political essays comprised my final current events exam. My father must have been amused when he read them, amused enough, anyhow, to keep them in his desk, where I found them after he'd died. One paper was a test answering four historical questions:

"What was the outcome of the Conference in Prague?"

"Which countries participated?"

"Tell us the difference in women's rights in Russia's bourgeois society vs. the Soviet Union's socialism?"

"What do you understand under an autarkist economy?"

The other essay explores this assigned topic: "German-Soviet Friendship Helps Us Build the DDR." I began with a quote from Stalin: "Hitlers come and go, the German people and the German state remain." Four hundred words later I end with this:

> It doesn't matter how many Wall Street strategists push war preparations and how many other peoples they misuse for cannon fodder. Together with the Soviet Union, the greatest bulwark of peace, we will fight for peace, and form an eternal bond of friendship with all peace-loving peoples.

Both papers got an "A." I can't remember Frau Döhner's grade for the dress. But she had taught me a lot about a craft I thoroughly loved. Frau Döhner had given me ever more challenging work and I had handled it all. But I had also learned that I might not have the imagination, the flair to be a top-notch designer. I certainly didn't want to be an ordinary seamstress or pattern cutter or fitter all of my life.

My parents organized a visit to Grandmama as a surprise birthday present. But at the last minute my father decided not to go. The continuing KGB surveillance made it just too risky for him to travel to the western sectors of Berlin. My mother asked me to come along instead.

Finally, my chance to buy fashionable shoes had arrived. The East Germans, and that included my family, still wore shoes made from a PVC-like material called Igelit. Truly awful stuff! Nobody who ever wore them will forget the feeling: cold and hard in the winter, hot and squishy in the summer. For months I had saved my DDR money. If I remember correctly, the exchange rate at that time was one West German mark to seven DDR marks.

The train to Berlin was packed with shoppers, all carrying empty suitcases. Our trip took place a decade before the Wall was built. There were checkpoints, but once in communist East Berlin, travel by train to the Western sector was still relatively easy. It turned out to be the last time I saw Grandmama alive, but I cannot remember a word we said to each other. I spent a lot of time in the West just window shopping, gawking and cruising the glitzy *Kurfürsten-dam*. Both the East and West sectors still had mountains of rubble, whole blocks with windowless buildings and churches without steeples. But in the West there were new shopping centers close to the U-Bahn (subway) stations. Around them the streets had been cleared and outdoor cafes beckoned with real coffee and cakes like *Alexander Torte* and *Berliner Pfannkuchen*. I was in seventh heaven just taking it all in. I quickly became convinced that I had to leave East Germany. I had no real roots. There would never be a future for me in the drab, depressing DDR.

When I found my red shoes, made from real leather with white crepe soles, they became the seal to my promise. I would leave my parents, Grandmama, Sonja, the dance halls and all of that.

On the train back, a group of East German police worked its way through the train. The sour-looking officers checked every-body's identifications, sometimes asking to see the contents of suit-cases. What were they looking for? I knew that certain items were not permitted. Would that include shoes? Or maybe there was a limit to how much each person was allowed to bring? When the police reached my mother and me, they looked at my shoes and asked to see the receipt.

"And what else did you buy?" A policewoman pointed to my little suitcase. There was nothing in it, except some dirty under-wear, my old Igelit shoes, a towel, soap and my toothbrush.

"You come with me," she said.

She took me to a lavatory and asked me to strip down. She checked my armpits and my crotch. She went through my hair, which I had piled into a bun on top of my head. I felt humiliated, a little scared.

Why had I been singled out? I'll never know. But I was flooded with relief and gratitude when it ended. She let me keep my new red shoes when she had had the power to ask me to take them off and put them on her own feet.

Chapter 14

I crossed the border from East to West Germany wearing my new red shoes with the white crepe soles. I could not pack them. What if my bag got lost?

Preparations took months, and were done in secrecy. Crossing the border was by now illegal, and political indoctrination was intense. I never knew which of my friends might denounce me and prevent me from leaving.

Aside from my parents, I only trusted Sonja. Did she want to come along? She surprised me with a dozen reasons no. She was an only child. She didn't want to leave her parents by themselves. Her father, an engineer, had successfully undergone de-Nazification and was ready to make a go at it with the new political regime. They had their own house. Sonja herself looked forward to a dental technician's career right there in Bitterfeld. She had a boyfriend. Sonja could not imagine leaving everything. Suddenly I saw how different our situations were. I was a refugee straddling fences, with no stake in East Germany. My prospects in the drab world of communist dress design looked dim. And I had glimpsed greener pastures in West Berlin.

My mother's reaction to my decision was another bout of depression. But my father understood. He worked to convince her that ultimately I had little future in the DDR. As a descendent of counter-revolutionary Baltic German nobility, I could most likely never make a real career. Father even went so far as to suggest that I might be persecuted once the new German communist regime hit full stride. Our family name collided with the new political climate. I wonder now if my father may have also worried that if I stayed any longer, the daily propaganda and my natural hopes for advancement might turn me into a communist.

I assured my mother that I would never leave her for good. I would merely be the first of us moving to the West. I naively imagined that once I had made my fortune as a dress designer, I would bring them both over and we would live in comfort and never be hungry again. I convinced myself that I really would become a star. All I needed was the chance.

With time, my mother accepted the idea and began to have thoughts of her own. My departure might create an opportunity for her to be reunited with her only sister, Mary. Tante Mary and Onkel Adolf now lived in Oberursel, near Frankfurt in West Germany.

In December of 1944, Onkel Adolf, a wounded veteran of World War I, was called back at the age of 51 to serve as an officer in the *Volksturm* defending an old fort in Poznan. Sometime around the beginning of February he was taken prisoner by the Red Army. He first worked in a stone quarry but was later promoted to designing new barracks for German prisoners. A highly infectious rash on his face most likely saved his life. His fellow prisoners were later to die wholesale of disease and malnutrition. But before that, Onkel Adolf developed terrible boils from using one of only two razors serving all the inmates in his prison camp. The Soviet guards grew so repulsed by the sight and vile smell of the running sores beneath his growing beard that they requested his release. Onkel Adolf was returned to Germany and rejoined his family in Oberursel in the fall of 1947.

My mother wrote coded letters to her sister and to her friends in the Zwingenberg Group. She had stayed in touch with them, all living in West Germany. They had sent us life-saving care packages when we were most desperate for high-calorie foods right after the war. Would they now give a helpful hand to get me established in the West? Our blood relatives, refugees like ourselves, were in no position to aid anybody. My mother mailed each letter from a different post office to avoid suspicion from the authorities. Weeks passed, but the coded responses trickled in and were encouraging. Everyone offered help in some way or another.

My own efforts centered on planning my escape. The Iron Curtain in 1951 still had loopholes. As my earlier trip with my mother to visit Grandmama makes clear, one route went through Berlin. Once we got past checkpoints into East Berlin, one had only to board the ring train, avoid police scrutiny, or snow them with a story if questioned, and one was soon in the West. But my mother had left my father behind as an implicit hostage. She and I also had a clear excuse in visiting an aged grandmother. This time I would be traveling alone, a prized young worker of nineteen, subject to much closer scrutiny. I would be unable to take a suitcase, which was then a dead giveaway to a planned escape. Mailing a case ahead to the West could be a giveaway too. Finally, if I did reach West Berlin, the authorities there had not yet set up reception centers. I lacked the money to pay my own plane ride to cities in the West where my family contacts resided.

Compared with these problems and risks, the nearby British-Soviet inter-zonal border looked attractive. It was barbed-wired in many places and patrolled by guards. But the DDR had yet to complete its infamous plowed death strip, mined and double barbed-wired on each side. The whole East German police state was still a work in progress. I had heard that crossing the border was easy. People seemed to be doing it every day, some to visit relatives and then returning to the East, others to stay permanently. Some took guides; others did it on their own.

Since I neither knew the terrain nor the best places to cross, I decided to find a guide. I cannot now recall all the details of my search. But eventually, a tipster whispered a name and address where I might find a good man in Magdeburg. I took a train the 40 miles to Magdeburg, made contact with this guide, sat in his kitchen, heard his pitch, and completed final arrangements. He just

seemed right. We set a day, time and place where we would meet
again. The place was a café near the railroad station of a secondary
train line going west out of Magdeburg. He said that there would
be other people there, some looking for guides, others just looking
for the best way to get across. He said that he would recruit others
there, and then we would cross at night into a well-lit open face
strip mine, busy with miners and dolly carts carrying coal. He liked
the idea of many people milling around the mine and on the slopes
of the slag mountains, which roughly formed the border between
East and West. Armed East German guards patrolled the border,
but they mostly stayed in widely spaced watchtowers. So it was usually easy to pass through the gaps. I paid him half his fee; the rest
he would collect on the other side. He was a man in his late thirties
with a big head of blond hair and claimed to have done this many
times before. I believed him.

Thus, on a mid-summer day in 1951, I came to say good-bye
to my parents. There was no bon voyage party and there were no
tears, just hugs and promises to write as soon as I was on the other
side. I remember my mother's last words: "Wherever you go and
whatever you do, remember the obligations of your inheritance.
Nobility has always been a privileged class. You have to act and behave better than anybody else."

Much later she told me that she cried for days. It was like losing another child.

Again I took the train from Bobbau to Magdeburg, and then
changed to the small commuter line that took me to the designated
station before the border. I found my man hanging out around the
entrance of the busy café. His height and sandy hair made him stick
out above everybody else. He told me to take a seat, talk to no one
and wait until it got dark. He would reappear and give a hand signal
for me to follow him. Then he left. I put my bag under my chair and
ordered an ersatz coffee. I had brought my own sandwich. Hours
passed in waiting and studying the scene in the small café. Each
train brought more people, all milling around. The café became

packed with men, women, children, suitcases, cigarette smoke and tension. A few were ordinary travelers. Others appeared to be guides trying to make a deal. Certainly we all wanted to appear as if we were on an outing. But families whispered anxiously while looking around for any signs of a police or border guard raid of the station.

The twilight deepened. My guide reappeared and raised his hand. The time had come. I followed him down a path. Behind a large group of bushes, we met the other clients he had assembled —a few short of a dozen. We huddled to hear his whispered instructions.

"Just follow me," he said. "Make yourself small and don't talk. When I say down, lie down. When I say run, run."

We set off slowly through woods, more or less single file, watching the ground so as not to stumble. It seemed pitch black, but in the distance I saw lights beaming up into the haze above the bottom of the strip mine. Some members of our group tripped and fell, and silently picked themselves up. The woods thinned. The black crest of the slag heaps loomed before us, etched against the lights from the mine. The guide whispered "down" and put a finger to his lips. We lay down and listened. Minutes passed. All I could hear was the beating of my heart and the grinding wheels of invisible railroad cars on curved tracks down in the mine. What if any of us had sneezed?

The guide rose, raising an arm. We stood and started forward. Fear choked the breath from my lungs. I had trouble carrying my bag. Suddenly it weighed a ton. I stumbled, not seeing where I was walking. Wordlessly, the guide reached over and took it himself. Our figures became visible in a half-light from the mine as we approached the rim. The rim. I was momentarily blinded looking into the lights flooding up from the works below. They illuminated a very steep descent. The guide started down, then I heard him shout, "Run!"

I ran. Down. I was taking short leaps down the steep slag toward the floodlights and moving trains. Down. Suddenly I heard gunshots. I felt the air of passing bullets on my cheeks. Or thought I did. *Run, Sigrid, run.* Down, down. The shots stopped as my strides flattened on the mine floor. I jumped over some tracks ahead of an oncoming coal train, clearing the locomotive but not the angry whistle of the engineer. He hung out his window, showering me with obscenities. My lungs were on fire.

With no breath left, I collapsed behind a bush. Where was I? Where was the guide and where was my bag? My bag! Not another person in sight. I was not sure where I was in relation to the border. In my panic and fear, I assumed I was still in the East. What was I going to do next?

Another train rattled by, filling the air with noise and white smoke. After it passed, I saw a man step out of a shadow some distance up the track and walk with determination towards me. He must be a guard sent to arrest me. I froze in fear. As he drew closer, I recognized the sandy mop of hair. My guide! Under the bright lights that mop looked more like a wig than hair. Maybe it was, I thought in distraction—you never knew what had happened to people during the Nazi and communist years. Or was it a disguise?

"Hello," he smiled. "I spotted your white socks and red shoes sticking out of the bush."

He held out my bag. It contained everything I owned that I was not wearing: my DDR identification card, 200 DDR Marks, 20 West German Marks, a change of underwear, a favorite sweater, a beloved skirt and blouse and a few other now forgotten items of clothing. My hero's sudden reappearance filled me with such relief that I almost fell into his arms.

"Where are we?" My heart rate made my voice tinny; my tongue felt inflated.

"You've made it. You're safe. We're in the West," he said.

Another huge wave of relief. Safe…safe. "But where are the others?" I finally asked.

"I really don't know. They're not here. I've searched the area. One of the miners said that a young girl was killed and the others gave up. I never expected shooting." He shook his head. "Maybe it was the girl in my group."

The guide led the way to the western railroad station. He was quite professional, making small talk, incredibly calm and reassuring despite the violence we had just survived. He also continued to carry my bag. "Maybe we'll find somebody else at the station," he said.

The small building served mainly the West German miners who commuted to their shifts. For a while we sat alone. Then other border crossers straggled in, but none from our group. We exchanged stories about how and where exactly we had crossed. They had also heard about a death, or maybe just a shooting. A noisy group of miners tramped in to await the first train to take them home. They excitedly reported the shooting of a woman or girl. Many other crossers were caught, they said. Apparently a new border crackdown had started just that night. The miners had grown used to safe crossings. Now they stared at us, marveling aloud at our luck. My guide finally abandoned hope of collecting the second half of his fee from any stragglers. It seemed there were not going to be any. He said he had to go back east to show up for his factory job in Magdeburg. I paid him and wished him good luck.

It puzzles me to this day why he felt it safe to return. Perhaps he had recruited the others in our group that very afternoon at that small rail station. So he had never given them his name. Perhaps he knew that the East German police would skip detailed interrogations. Or perhaps he had paid off the guards. Maybe his blond mop really was a wig. Anyhow, he left the station and walked east that night, and I shuddered at his courage.

At daybreak I joined the miners on the train. I was still numb from the shock of my narrow escape. But I also felt happy. I was out. And one of my mother's friends from the Zwingenberg Group, Fräulein Schmitt, was waiting for me in Braunschweig, 25 miles away. She had kindly offered a stay for a few days before I entered a camp to get my official papers for permanent residency in the *Bundesrepublik*.

I remember my time with Fräulein Schmitt for two events. One was the weekend I spent on my first—highly informal—job in the West. Fräulein Schmitt's best friend, director of a home for wayward girls, needed a substitute supervisor over the weekend. I nervously agreed to be the stand-in. The girls in the home were almost as old as I. The police called me the first night to come to their station and pick up one of our wards. They had arrested her getting drunk in a bar in the inner city. I was frightened that the police might ask me for a West German ID. But I signed her out without being questioned and brought her back.

My second memory, equally bizarre, is of my first taste of American Coca-Cola. The drink had been touted as a great, enslaving capitalist evil by East German propaganda. I didn't just sip my first Coke; I swigged it down directly from the bottle, feeling truly to have arrived. Arrived in the real world drinking straight from a bottle! Imagine. Not from a glass. I have never told anybody, but not only did I not know how to drink from a bottle—the stuff dribbled down my chin—but the Coca-Cola tasted awful.

I became a legal resident of West Germany at the *Notaufnahmelager* (Emergency Reception Camp) in Uelzen-Bohldam in August of 1951. The very important document said, "By her personal testimony, the applicant was able to prove that she could no longer reside in the Soviet Occupation Zone." I cannot remember now the tale of persecution or grievance that I told to obtain this official ruling. But with that document in hand, I said goodbye to the East, to Lenin, Stalin, Pieck and their comrades forever. Whatever my problems in the future, I knew for a certainty that I never wanted to go back there.

The major highways in Germany in the early 1950s were clogged with young people raising their thumbs. Alongside the Autobahn particularly, men and women competed for a chance to get picked up by a commercial truck, an American military vehicle, or by the few drivers fortunate enough to own a Volkswagen, Opel or Mercedes. With my new West German passport in hand, I

pulled on my red shoes and hiked out to the Autobahn in Braunschweig, looking for a ride south. Soon a huge box van pulled up
with the name Bahlsen, a famous bakery, stenciled on its side. I
climbed aboard. The friendly driver said that he was going as far as
Frankfurt with his first delivery. When he heard that I had not
eaten a Bahlsen cookie since the war, he gave me a box of butter
cookies.

Hundreds of thousand of refugees just like me languished in
barracks in refugee camps all over Germany—some had been
there since the late forties. But thanks to my mother, the three suc-
cessive rides I hitched that day took me to a job that had been offered by the husband of one of her friends. Dr. Mischlich was a
general practitioner with a large practice in and around Zwingenberg near Darmstadt. My job was to keep track of insurance forms
and assist the doctor with patients at the ground floor practice in
the Mischlichs' large house. He promised a modest salary, and Frau
Mischlich found an inexpensive attic room for me in a nearby private home. Settling in, I felt vindicated about my decision to come
to the West. Everything was going to be great. Zwingenberg was
not just anywhere. It straddled an historic road, the Bergstrasse,
dating back to the Romans at least, and was famous for its half-
timber houses and its fruit tree blossom festivals in the spring.

I loved the white nurse's apron. It covered up my shabby East
German clothes. I learned to sterilize needles and instruments and
to give inter-muscular injections. To acquire the right touch, Dr.
Mischlich asked me to practice on a small pillow, tightly stuffed
with kapok. Pop. No…Pop! On most weekends, I hitchhiked my
way to Oberursel, just off the Autobahn north of Frankfurt, to
visit Onkel Adolf, Tante Mary and their children, Karin, Gertrud
and Wolfgang. Being refugees themselves, they had limited space
in their rented ground floor apartment. But they were always willing to feed one more mouth and let me sleep in their living room
on a folding cot.

My work with Dr. Mischlich ended abruptly eight months

later. I had grown increasingly aware that the job in a small town was getting me no closer to my dream of dress design. This was not on my mind, however, as Dr. Mischlich and I drove back one fine spring day from a house call in a nearby village. The apple trees were in full bloom and the Volkswagen's windows were rolled down to admit the fragrant air. Dr. Mischlich shifted gears. His hand wound up on my thigh. He looked at me, lust filling his eyes.

My initial panic gave way to anger. What was he thinking? I yanked my leg away. Should I tell his wife or even my mother? Out of the question. They would never hear about it. I would deal with this. I suddenly asked myself, "What am I doing in Zwingenberg anyway? And now I'm being pawed by an old married man." I decided to quit on the spot when the car reached home.

The next day I said goodbye to the Mischlichs, to the apple blossoms, to my attic room, and marched once again to the Autobahn. I hitched to Oberursel and temporary refuge.

For days, I agonized over my next move. I faced one huge reality. A career as a fashion designer was out of the question. I had no financial means to study at a design school. Now that I had seen the sleek styles in the West, I also secretly wondered if I had enough talent to be a designer. Anyhow, I'd never be able to find out. I surely did not want to go back as a seamstress with a dressmaker. One troubling personal concern existed as well. The American Zone was a bright world away from the sad Soviet Zone of Occupation. But I was still a refugee, a stranger, with no prospects in a land far from home. I did not really want to be here. Maybe America?

In the midst of this personal crisis, I heard from my parents that Grandmama had died in Berlin. She had fallen and broken a leg while taking her daily walk. From the hospital Grandmama had dictated a typically haughty postcard. An excerpt:

> May 22, 1952
> Dear Children,
> …My leg is in a cast but I have no pain.…I'm well taken

care of but if I'm being neglected, I use the old aristocratic approach of creating a scene. It always brings results without resentment. I have two agreeable roommates and the doctor comes every day for 2 seconds...

Hugs from Omchen (little grandma), it's what they call me here.

Grandmama developed pneumonia. Penicillin was not yet available, and she died on June 3rd, three months short of her 90th birthday. Her remains were cremated and, according to her wishes, buried next to Grandpapa's in Ahrenshoop. I did not attend. I feared that going back to communist East Germany might be held against me if I decided to immigrate to the U.S. Besides, Grandmama did not come to my confirmation and I'm sure she would not have come to my funeral, if I should have died before her.

Unable to figure my future, I hitched a ride a few weeks later to Wiesbaden to consult an old friend of my father's, Helmut Brümmer-Patzig. He and his actress wife had often visited us in Majkow. He was the confident U-Boat captain from World War I and shore officer in World War II. It was he who in 1943 had shocked Grandmama by uttering these words first: "Hitler is doomed and so is his war." Now it was my turn to be bold. I mentioned to them that I might want to immigrate to America. The more I'd thought about it, I felt ready. In my 22nd year I was old enough for a new beginning in a foreign land. Forgotten were my earlier promises to help my parents settle in the West. I was only thinking about myself. Besides, my vision of achieving riches through dress design had been a pipe dream.

"Why not Canada?" Brümmer-Patzig asked, not questioning the idea of immigration. "Your brother is there, isn't he? And so are some relatives of your mother?"

"Yes, but they all live in the country, working on farms," I said. "Ulf's in a mine somewhere in the north of Canada." Canada appeared drab in comparison to America. "I want to live in New York," I added, "or maybe San Francisco."

"I can understand that," he said, a world traveler himself. "But if you're serious, you must first perfect your spoken English. I'll finance your Berlitz classes. You can pay me back once you become a millionaire in America.

"You should also learn to play bridge," he added. "Once in New York it will open doors to you to meet the right American society."

That visit crystallized my decision. America it was to be.

Chapter 15

A visit to the American Consulate in Frankfurt dashed my excitement. The tiny annual quota of visas for Estonian citizens, established in 1924, was filled for decades to come. Even though I was now a German citizen, I could not apply under the vastly larger German quota. One's place of birth was all that mattered under U.S. law. A consulate official suggested I try for a visa under the Refugee Relief Act of 1948. It provided 400,000 extra visas for post-war refugees from countries behind the Iron Curtain, like me. My hopes jumped. The official checked, then came back to say that the quota under the Act had been filled. And so, sadly—just now —was the waiting list. There remained only one distant glimmer of light. Congress was considering passage of a new refugee relief act.

I still wanted to go to America. It wasn't just what I read in newspapers and magazines and what I saw about America in the movies. My experience hitching rides with American soldiers had also impressed me. I liked their friendliness, casualness and general happy-go-lucky attitudes—they seemed a new kind of people. But now I still needed a job. Maybe, I thought, I could draw a paycheck and improve my high school English by getting work with the American forces.

The U.S. Army Civilian Personnel Section in Frankfurt turned out to have openings. I first had to complete a crash course in typing, English and military correspondence. I graduated at 42 English words per minute on December 1, 1952. Six weeks later I started as a document clerk for the Engineer Procurement Center of the

7741st Army Unit in Frankfurt. With the employment came an astonishing bonus in housing-short Germany. I was assigned three whole rooms, plus shared kitchen and bath, in a magnificent townhouse commandeered by American occupying forces. The circumstances reminded me, weirdly, of my family's situation in Poland, where the Nazis had commandeered first the villa in Poznan and later Majkow so that we could live there. My mother had worried deeply about the fate of the prior owners. I never gave a thought to the owner of my new apartment. Years later, on a visit to Frankfurt, my husband and I encountered this man busy gardening in his front yard. When I identified myself as being a tenant during the occupation, he showered us Americans with wrath.

"Without the Russians you would never have beaten us," he said.

The typing pool at the Engineer Procurement Center cranked out a blizzard of orders for spare parts for military vehicles, nuts and bolts and other supplies. We were supervised by a sergeant who sat at a big empty desk, similar to a teacher at the head of a class. His sole function was to make sure that we did not goof off too much in the washroom or talk too much among ourselves. I still remember the sight of him, always chewing gum, his feet on the desk and his face in an issue of *Stars and Stripes* or a well-worn comic book. Hour after hour, a picture of pitiful boredom.

My job with the Americans did give me the opportunity for the first time to enjoy independence and to sample something close to normal life. I bought my own fabrics and sewed a new wardrobe. I began to date. I could afford to bring an occasional present to the Ronnefeldts when I spent my weekends with them. I hitchhiked to Paris in 1953 for a visit with my cousin Karin, who was then a student at one of the prestigious fashion design schools. Here and there I even picked up an odd lesson in the game of bridge.

Late that fall, I met an American soldier at a cocktail party given by Terry Nossis, a new friend. Terry, an American civilian working for an Army intelligence unit, liked inviting a mix of Germans and Americans. The soldier, Rich Thomas, wore civilian clothes, drove a civilian car and was stationed in her unit. We began dating, and in early 1954 he told me that President Dwight Eisenhower had signed the new refugee law half a year before.

The Refugee Relief Act of 1953 provided 214,000 new visas for displaced persons from the East. I quickly filed my papers. Each applicant, however, faced an exhausting background check. The law was passed during the height of American McCarthyism. It barred anyone who had a criminal record, had been a prostitute, had active tuberculosis, had a record as a Nazi, or had ever been a communist, anarchist or other subversive. Since all of the eligible refugees, by definition, had spent most of their lives behind what was then the Iron Curtain, these background checks would take many months, even years.

The law also required that each applicant find an American sponsor who would guarantee a job or promise to support the refugee for the first year if she or he did not find work. Many immigrants were sponsored by religious organizations, others by U.S. businesses seeking employees. My sponsorship problem was solved, almost miraculously, at one of Terry Nossis' parties. There I met a widow, Alice Kandarian, from Worchester, Massachusetts, who was returning from a short vacation in Europe to the United States. I was amazed when she offered to sponsor me after a short conversation. I didn't quite believe my luck. But we met for breakfast the next day, and she hadn't changed her mind.

"Just mail me the forms," she said. "My own parents immigrated to the States from Armenia many years ago."

This generous American later was as good as her word, signing papers that in theory at least committed her to support me for a year—all this based on one conversation at a party.

My cousin Karin, who also wanted to immigrate to the States, had already received her visa under the native German quota. With much envy I saw her leave that spring with a ticket on a luxury liner. In her pocket she carried a list of contacts she might look up in

New York City. Among them was the phone number of Dave Thomas, Rich Thomas' older brother, now working for *Life* magazine. Karin promised I could stay with her when I came myself.

I wrote my parents in East Germany in coded letters about my plans. They were strangely distant. What I didn't know was that my father was having problems of his own. My parents wrote me only about happy events—their mail could be opened. The Soviet Army had turned the Agfa Film Factory in Wolfen over to the East German government in the spring of 1954. My father was fifty-six years old and had a good job there. But now the political protection he had enjoyed as an employee of the Soviet occupiers disappeared. East Germany's communist party, the SED (*Sozialistische Einheitspartei Deutschlands*), within months began politically evaluating the work force. As my father wrote in a subsequent affidavit,

> My position (under the SED) became increasingly difficult, because of my family's class and origins. There was no doubt in their minds about my political opinion of their regime. In addition they knew that my son was in Canada and my daughter in Frankfurt was working for the U.S. Army.

A friend in a private Baltic German organization in West Berlin had already warned Father that Baltic nobles living in East Germany might be facing some kind of roundup. Now his co-workers started passing warnings that they were being asked about his political views. Though reluctant to face once again a whole new start in life, he began planning a departure. The East German regime had adopted a fairly liberal travel policy for citizens over 55. These workers would be claiming state pensions soon. Their defection would relieve the socialist state of rising health care burdens too. So departure of the elderly, though a political loss, was an economic gain. My father, as long as he left my mother behind, was able to obtain a three-month interzonal pass. With the political pressure increasing, he quit his job at the Agfa factory at the end of March 1955 and traveled to Wiesbaden, where he stayed with his friend

Helmut Brümmer-Patzig. Once there, he got a doctor to issue him a medical diagnosis of bronchitis with orders to stay in a hospital.

I learned all this only when my father called me on the phone from Wiesbaden. We shared a joyful reunion—and saw each other often over the next few months. He in fact seemed healthy and was never hospitalized. But he sent additional medical documents to my mother. These enabled her to get his travel pass extended until the fall. It kept his options open. But Mother nonetheless started packing their valuables and belongings into relatively small boxes and shipping them to Wiesbaden, never from the same post office twice.

In August the police started knocking at my mother's door. They demanded to know when her husband was getting back, even though his medically extended interzonal pass was still valid. They showed up once or twice a week after that asking the same question. Mother managed to mail several more packages. Then in late September rumors linked to the Sachsen-Anhalt state police reached her. The Soviet Union, it was said, had supplied the police with lists of persons born in the Baltic states who were now living in East Germany. Under Soviet law, they were now Soviet, not East German, citizens. The Baltic Germans were soon to be taken into custody and "voluntarily" repatriated to the countries of their birth.

Repatriation east, for my father at least, would have meant at best a Siberian labor camp. Maybe even a firing squad, since he had fought against the Soviets in 1920. In my mother's last coded postcard, she wrote in Estonian that she had mailed all the packages and would now visit cousin Maud, the code name for Berlin. Then she fled herself to West Berlin, where the German government by then had opened a refugee reception center.

In the midst of all this, my visa came through, along with assignment to a September berth on the *USS General Langfitt*. This was one of several U.S. Army troop ships pressed into service to provide cut-rate transportation for refugees like me to America. The visa actually came down more quickly than I had expected. In my spare time, I started furiously sewing custom dresses for American officers' wives. I needed the money to help pay my passage.

I never saw my mother before I left for America. She reached the Berlin refugee center on October 10 and was flown for processing to a refugee camp in Hanau, near Frankfurt. For my parents, this was their fourth forced relocation since 1926, when Father had lost Avanduse to the land reform in Estonia. They were once again impoverished, starting all over from scratch. But they hoped at least to spend the rest of their lives in a free country where they did have a few relatives and friends. And they were safe.

I was wearing a pair of fashionable high heel pumps when I climbed into a third class train compartment in Frankfurt in September of 1955, bound for the port city of Bremen. I was not going to the USS *General Langfitt* and on to New York wearing my old red shoes. I had long ago thrown them out. I felt no sadness leaving Germany or Europe. That was the past. Adventure, the future. I cradled the same excitement I had had when leaving Majkow ten years earlier. As the train rumbled out of the city, I gazed from the swaying window onto the flat fall landscape of northern Germany. But my mind was already in America, in New York City. I had everything I thought I needed for my new beginning right there in my speckled brown cardboard suitcase, reinforced with metal corners.

I had prepared for the trip alone. But I was just one person in a wave of hundreds of thousands migrating from Europe that year and the next. My arrival at the U.S. Army transport service reception center in Bremen-Lesum shocked me into this awareness. Vast dormitories and mess halls housed and served hundreds of noisy families dressed mostly in Eastern European clothes. I had not seen so many drab and worried-looking people in one place since leaving the DDR. Many had come straight from displaced persons camps, where they had often waited for years, receiving West German and international aid. When I later read the verses of Emma Lazarus about the Statue of Liberty, "Send me your tired, your poor, your huddled masses..." my mind flashed back to scenes from those drafty halls in Bremen-Lesum. We bunked six women to a room and shuffled from tables to desks to other tables getting our papers checked, our sleeping berths assigned and our boarding instructions. Refugees with some education and languages helped those without these advantages to get their papers in order. I helped two women in my bunk room who spoke only Polish and Yiddish and another who could not write or read at all. The shower facilities came in row upon row of eight open stalls for all the women in the camp. Initially I was too embarrassed to undress in front of so many strangers. Get over it, an attendant said, the *USS General Lang-fitt* would have the same arrangement.

Two days later we were bused to a wharf in Bremerhaven, where, under overcast skies, I climbed up the gangway of our gray troop carrier. I remembered my boarding of Hitler's *Ozeana* in Tallinn more than fifteen years earlier. The *Langfitt*, at 9,950 tons, was double the size, but the makeup of the milling passengers was the same, mostly families with young children and teenagers, and very few singles. In contrast to the *Ozeana*'s passengers, however, these families spoke a dozen different languages. Russian, Yiddish, Polish, Hungarian I recognized, but many others I had never heard before. Only a few spoke a decent German; almost none spoke English. For most of this trip I stayed mainly to myself.

Women and men bunked separately in low-ceilinged compartments. These came equipped with rows of pipe sleeping racks. Hammocks were lashed between the piping to provide a depressed sleeping surface from which it was difficult to roll out. The hammocks were stacked three high, one on top of another. Teenagers and young women were assigned top berths, which could only be reached by a steep ladder. My hammock was so close to the ceiling that I could barely sit up. Young children bunked with their mothers. Men were not allowed in the women's compartments; they were only to meet in the common rooms. The congestion was indescribable. These spaces may have been fit for disciplined soldiers, but anybody who could squeeze out to some other part of the ship during daytime did so. Our compartment was below the water line, dimly lit by a few blue light bulbs. Cafeteria meals came in brightly scrubbed aluminum trays with compartments for soup, meat, potatoes, vegetables and dessert. The servings were huge, and until we hit the open sea, they all disappeared in a hurry. A nursery and kindergarten cared for small children in what seemed the very bottom of the ship.

Adults and teenagers did have one common lounge to themselves in the superstructure. Bolts held all chairs, tables and some easy chairs firmly to the floor. Up against one wall I found a rack packed with well-fingered pocket books and outdated magazines, all in English. I pulled out a magazine called *The New Yorker*. After all, that's where I was going. But much to my dismay I could neither understand the cartoons nor comprehend the text of the articles. And here I thought that I could read and understand English. How was I going to find a job when I couldn't even understand a joke?

Shortly after leaving port, I witnessed a happy celebration. The Jewish passengers aboard all entered the mess hall one day laughing, embracing and kissing one another. They sat down to an unusually boisterous meal. Somebody explained that it was their New Year, Rosh Hashanah. Their gaiety reminded me of all my own New Year celebrations I had spent in the past.

I began hanging around the bridge tables hoping that one of the grim-looking men would make me an offer to join. But none were interested. They enjoyed screaming at their male bridge buddies in languages I did not understand.

Everything changed abruptly in the mid-Atlantic. We ran into a storm with hurricane-strength gusts of wind. Nobody was allowed on deck. The ship seemed half submerged in water. The engines slowed dramatically, and the captain turned the ship's head to the oncoming seas. The loudspeakers in due course passed the word that the storm would delay us getting into New York City. Within hours, our mess hall was almost deserted. The steam tables stayed untouched; the kitchen personnel in their white sanitary caps stood idly gossiping among themselves. We few who came out for dinner had to hold on to our trays and flatware as we ate; the storm rails around the tables were too low to contain our utensils.

Most passengers stayed in their hammocks, too sick to move about by day or night. When wives did not show up for dinner, some worried husbands came to look for them at night. My compartment turned into a zoo. I heard screams of mistaken identities as the men were feeling bodies and calling out names of their loved ones. Eventually the husbands were chased out by the ship's crew. The storm that had sickened me long ago on the *Ozeana* now seemed a picnic. This time I never became ill outright, feeling mostly nauseous, sometimes a little or sometimes a lot. The first night was terrifying.

I know that millions have traveled through storms at sea. But to this day I believe doing it in the bowels of a troop compartment packed with seasick women and children is special. The howling of the wind mixed with the random boom of waves banging our sides and the constant groaning of the hull plates and the slamming and rolling of the ship. All this I endured in a steel box jammed with baggage and dozens of moaning bodies and lit with those weird blue lights. I grew certain that I was going to die lying in my hammock. It could happen any moment. I imagined the ship's plates giving way to a huge wall of water bursting into our cabin. Oblivion. It surely seemed the end.

When morning finally, finally arrived, I was amazed to be alive. Reluctantly I made it up to the lounge, holding onto the railings, sometimes even being lifted off the deck by a violent movement of the ship. The lounge was nearly empty now, except for one bridge table of four. By the afternoon there were only three. They called over and asked in broken German if I wanted to join them in a game. I eagerly accepted. But these men were experts. They now had somebody new and truly incompetent to scream at. Scream they did, while clutching their heads in dismay.

"Why did you do this?…Unbelievable… The most stupid bid … Only a woman would do this kind of thing!"

It was painful, but I stuck it out, glad to have something to do. I had actually learned a little bridge by the time the hurricane blew out.

We were three days late, and twelve days out of Bremerhaven, when the first seagulls circled the *General*, signaling the approach of land. The word spread fast. The ship's loudspeaker announced that early next morning we would pass the Statue of Liberty and dock in New York Harbor. I don't think that anyone on the ship had much sleep that night. I, for one, was so excited, but also nervous, that I just lay in my hammock thinking about what it was going to be like.

I was on deck even before the sun rose to reserve a place up front at the port side rail. This was the best place to see both the statue and New York, I had been told by the ship's crew. The railings filled up around me, one, two and then many layers deep. The murmuring of the crowd in the darkness overrode the sound of the throbbing engines of the ship. The eastern sky turned silver, and then I saw land. With the rising of the morning sun, the *General Langfitt* split the New York Narrows. The Statue of Liberty came into view. A few people cheered. Then I glanced ahead and saw the New York skyline.

There it was! Even bigger than I had imagined! Pink light from the rising sun spotlighted the soaring towers and twinkled from hundreds of windows. The sky beyond was still dark gray. Everyone aboard our ship had seen photos of this fabled pyramid of buildings. But like the Grand Canyon, seeing the real thing with your own eyes is entirely different.

The sight of this awesome spectacle floating on the waters evoked from our ship of immigrants a mighty, united howl.

A U.S. Army transport, like the *Langfitt*, arrives in New York harbor with 800 refugees.

Epilogue

I cannot end this story without addressing the moral issues raised by my family's flight through the 20th century. Any German or ethnic German who lived under the Nazi regime has a personal accounting to make. This truth has faded over time, but it returned to sharp focus recently with the publication in 2006 of the memoir *Peeling the Onion,* by Günter Grass. Mr. Grass, Germany's greatest living novelist, won the Nobel Prize in 1970. He has played the role of Germany's public conscience ever since, scolding ex-Nazis and warning of fascist tendencies in Germany and in the U.S. In *Peeling the Onion,* Mr. Grass startled the world by revealing, for the very first time, that he himself, at age seventeen, had served not just in the German army but in a Nazi unit, the Waffen SS, in 1945. Mr. Grass was drafted like most youths his age. But he admits that he was a zealous teenage Nazi and went eagerly to war against the Red Army. Mr. Grass was heavily criticized for hypocrisy in delaying for so long the confession of his armed, if youthful, complicity in fascism.

I have far less baggage. I was thirteen, four years younger than Mr. Grass, when Hitler's war ended. No personal doubts trouble me about my behavior. Just to be liked, I went along with almost anything that my friends and teachers suggested. I never felt responsible for what Hitler was doing. I never thought of informing against friends or grownups as we students were encouraged to do by one of our teachers. This was not out of opposition to Nazism. It was just something no member of my family was supposed to do. Maybe by 1944 or 1945 I should have begun asking questions.

But I was aware that asking a question in school was vaguely dangerous. At home, my parent's tight-lipped silence about politics shut off questions too. My father and mother must have talked among themselves, but I don't even know that for certain. In conversation, my parents' generation was far less open with themselves or with their children than is the present generation.

What I do know is this: I owe my life, while escaping from Poland, to young soldiers like Günter Grass. And I survived the hideous slaughter of the war. Millions of Jewish, Polish, Russian, German and other children exactly like me did not. For that I am grateful, and humbled.

I am aware that some guilt may be laid upon my parents. After escaping first Lenin and then Stalin, they passed through, and exploited to the full, the Nazi dismemberment of Poland. My father helped survey Polish agricultural estates for the Nazi party after Germany's victory in 1939. Then he managed Majkow, one of the estates that the Nazis handed out to German or ethnic German colonists. We prospered right up to the time that we left in January of 1945. On the other hand, my parents were the most reluctant of colonists. They would have stayed in Estonia had there been any choice. Once in Poland, my father inherited a harsh and drunken estate overseer from the Polish owners of Majkow. Why did my father not know how bad he was and keep this man? Again, I did not ask, even though I disliked and feared Mr. Kerinski. Yet my father was personally considerate of the Polish families and workers on the estate. They helped us in the orderly packing of our belongings down to the day of departure. Some even cried. Four of our Polish coachmen drove us out of our gate as we started our trek. And when they returned to protect their families the next day, they left us with all our belongings, most of our horses, food and feed.

I never discussed any of these issues with my parents after the war. I know that they felt no responsibility for Hitler. He rose to power long before they left Estonia. They never supported him by joining the party. This was an act of defiance among colonists in Poland, and it brought my father briefly to a Nazi re-education camp in the fall of 1944. But my parents never actively opposed Hitler either. If anything, my mother and father felt themselves to be pawns of history. Hitler represented one in a series of dismal events in their lives that they had no hand in creating. My parents met each challenge and survived. Guilt or shame seemed beside the point. As my father often put it, "What could one do?"

A final judgment of the moral ambiguities in our story is left to the reader.

Collective guilt just for being an ethnic German hit me only when I arrived in New York City in 1955. I worked briefly as a dressmaker in a fashion couture shop in Manhattan. Then I landed a job, first as a trainee and next as a film editor, for *Life* magazine. Many staff photographers were Holocaust survivors. My heavy German accent immediately tabbed me as a suspect. Who could blame them? For the first time I felt guilty about the war. Alfred Eisenstaedt, one of *Life*'s most celebrated photographers and a Holocaust survivor, flatly told my superior that he did not want "this Nazi" to edit any of his pictures. The ban by Eisie, as he was affectionately called, lasted two years.

Then suddenly he acknowledged one day that I was a fine editor and that he would not mind me handling his work. I never asked for reasons. Maybe he found out that I was born in Estonia, or that I had never lived in Germany during the war, or that I was only thirteen when the war ended. Maybe my professionalism won him over. But Eisie's change of mind, when it came, redeemed me as a person even more than as an editor. I felt immense relief. Single-handedly, he had freed me from a terrible burden. In later years, Eisie went back to Germany to visit his hometown, where a documentary film was made of the event. It had its premier showing at the Smithsonian Institution in Washington, D.C. For opening night in October of 1980, Eisie sent me a personal invitation.

My parents eventually settled in an unfurnished apartment in Oberursel, a small town in the foothills of the Taunus Mountains, outside Frankfurt. They wound up renting their rooms from my old benefactors, Tante Mary and Onkel Adolf. By then, the Ronnefeldts had acquired a townhouse in a new development. This happy landing of my parents marked a turnaround after several grim years. Their new start in West Germany was in many ways the hardest of the four new beginnings that rocked their lives. Fifty-eight when he arrived, my father had to scramble for odd jobs until he turned sixty and could qualify for West German support. One post was as a tour guide at the site of a Stone Age village being excavated in north Germany. When Father failed to find work, which was often, he took solace in his garden or checked out the local dump. Though living in a new apartment, my parents did not have the means to buy even used furniture or household utensils. The dump yielded pots, pans, chipped plates, cups and saucers and furniture. My father especially prized two dining room chairs with all four legs intact, a little round table, a bookcase and a genuine silver cream pitcher. It was badly tarnished and full of dents, but he had it restored to its original beauty. My mother delighted in this one piece of luxury, but wondered who in their right mind would throw silver into the trash.

In desperation for an income, my mother eventually took a job as a maid for a well-to-do family in Frankfurt. Her employers quickly discovered that my mother had no idea how to clean a house or cook a proper meal. The kind-hearted couple then did an unusual thing. They kept her on to tend to fresh flowers and plants inside and outside their house. To do the cleaning and cooking, they hired another woman.

Everything started to look up after my father reached sixty. He began receiving a small pension from the West German government to compensate for the losses my parents had suffered in abandoning their home, business and investments in Estonia. (West

Germany made a heroic effort to offer some compensation to all German refugees from the east.) There was even enough in my parents' stipend to permit them to do a little touring by bus. My father's garden plot near their new apartment became a little Eden. To the delight of his new friends, he again became the Tomato Baron. He grew fruit, vegetables and a wide variety of tomatoes from seeds that he brought back from trips with my mother to Greece and Spain.

After my mother died at the age of seventy-nine, my father married again. As noted in Chapter 13, it was not Helene von Voigt, who outlived him by several years and also died in the West. My father married, instead, Sylvia Starke, a vivacious, retired teacher. She had saved a lot of money and drove a Mercedes. Sylvia and my father soon visited my husband and me in Maryland, where he instantly fell in love with the wildness of the American countryside.

"If I were a young man again and I could not live in Estonia," he wrote, "I would like to come to America. The enormous variety of native plants growing in the mountains and near the shoreline of the East Coast is just overwhelming. And, of course, I could grow whole new varieties of tomatoes."

My father died in May of 1979, at the age of eighty-two, following a stroke suffered on holiday in the Canary Islands. He is buried in the *Waldfriedhof* (Forest Cemetery) of Oberursel, where he is flanked by my mother on one side and Sylvia on the other.

My brother Ulf immigrated to Canada in 1950. After years of back-wrenching work in mines and meat packing plants, he trained himself as a photographer. He later built a fine career as a criminal photo specialist at the Forensic Laboratory of the Solicitor General of Ontario. In that position he authored several research reports printed in the *Journal of Forensic Sciences*. Ulf married a refugee from Germany, anglicized his name to Alf, and now lives in a suburb of Toronto. To the grief of my parents, Ulf remained distant from them until they died. My own relationship with him has not been close.

My cousin Karin Ronnefeldt quickly rose to the top as a designer of cocktail and evening dresses in New York City. Her evening gowns filled all the windows at Bergdorf Goodman's at Christmas time of 1955. She put me up in her apartment when I arrived on the *Langfitt* and arranged my first job as a dressmaker in her studio. Karin had contacted Rich Thomas's brother, Dave, for aid in polishing the professional resume that helped her land her position. Dave was a reporter at *Life*. They instantly fell in love and were married in New York City the following year. The couple now lives in Camden, Maine. It was Dave, incidentally, who got me my first interview with *Life*.

I lost track of Grandmama's companion, Fräulein Lukas. But my mother stayed in touch. Much later she told me that Fräulein Lukas' marriage was not altogether happy; Herr Motte was a good provider but an alcoholic.

My life in New York moved rapidly from immigrant with cardboard suitcase to a career at *Life*. It had many thrilling moments. One was unique. The date was November 22, 1963. It was around midnight, and all of *Life*'s top editors had jammed into the magazine's photo lab to get their first look at a long, long strip of 8 mm color movie film. It was fresh from a rush development job in the magazine's dark room. *Life* had acquired exclusive first publication rights to this film, which was shot by an amateur photographer named Abraham Zapruder. That day, Zapruder had stood at the side of a street on Dealey Plaza in Dallas, Texas, as a motorcade bearing President John F. Kennedy rolled past. Shots rang out and Zapruder kept filming. We editors now looked at the filmstrips on our light tables, not believing what we saw. These now-famous photos remain the only ones taken showing the actual assassination of President Kennedy.

Rich Thomas returned from Europe in December of 1955, and I married him a year later in New York City. We detoured briefly to Ann Arbor, Michigan, where Rich took up and then dropped graduate studies. We were soon back in New York, pursuing journalistic careers, mine at *Life* and his at the *New York Post* and then later at *Newsweek* magazine. In 1970, Rich was transferred to Washington, D.C., where we now still live. Our children, Karina and Stryk, are out on their own.

In this book, I adopt the names of cities, villages and manor houses in Estonia and Poland that are in use today. For the sake of the historical record, the following list records the German names of the same places.

Estonian/German Place Names

Avanduse	Awandus
Haapsalu	Hapsal
Imavere	Immafer
Kapu	Kappo
Kaserahu	Birkenruh
Keila Joa	Schloss Fall
Nõmme	Nõmme
Paldiski	Baltischport
Rakvere	Wesenberg
Rutikvere	Ruttigfer
Simuna	St. Simonis
Tallinn	Reval
Tartu	Dorpat
Udriku	Uddrich
Venevere	Wennefer
Võivere	Woibifer
Võnnu	Wenden

Polish/German Place Names

Droszkow	Droskau
Glogów	Glogau
Kalisz	Kalisch
Leszno	Lissa
Lódz	Lodsch/Litzmannstadt
Mayakouskoye	Nemersdorf
Poznan	Posen
Szczecin	Stettin
Zagan	Sagan

Photograph Credits

All photographs are from the author's personal collection with the exception of the following:

p. 30: from Archiv der Deutschbalten Kulturstiftung, Luneberg
pp. 156, 161 from the National Archives
p. 229 from the National Archives for the New York *Daily Mirror*

Reproduction Rights

Cassell Pic, a division of the Orion Publishing Group Ltd. (London), granted kind permission for the quotations from *The Road to Berlin*, by John Erickson, appearing in Chapter 10.

The names and identifying characteristics of some people featured in this book have been changed to protect their privacy. Any resemblance between such names and identifying characteristics and those of other persons, living or dead, is coincidental.

Cartography by Philip Schwartzberg, Meridian Mapping, Minneapolis
Cover design: Eric Lindsey
Interior design: Jennifer Adkins

Book Clubs

Telephone interviews or e-mail sessions can be arranged with the author by calling 301-299-7093.

Bibliography

Bielenstein-Bosse, Barbara, and Bosse, Peter-Joachen. *Auch wir verliessen das Land...Die Umsiedlung der Deutschbalten 1939-1941*. Neuthor Verlag, 1989.

Bremen, Carl von. *Kinder am Meer*. Hubert Stuffer Verlag. Berlin, 1933.

Bruemmer, Fred. *Survival—A Refugee Life*. Key Porter Books Ltd. Toronto, 2005.

Burleigh, Michael. *The Third Reich*. Hill and Wang, Division of Farrar, Straus and Giroux. New York, 2000.

Erickson, John, Dr. *The Road to Berlin*. Harper & Row. New York, 1983.

Grass, Günter. *Peeling the Onion*. Harcourt Books. New York, 2007.

Hunt, Irmgard A. *On Hitler's Mountain—Overcoming the Legacy of a Nazi Childhood*. Harper Collins, New York, 2005.

Keegan, John. *The Second World War*. Penguin Books, 1990.

Knopp, Guido. *Die Grosse Flucht*. Verlag Ullstein, 2002.

Kühnel, Horst. *Die Deutschen im Baltikum—Geschichte und Kultur. Fünf Aufträge*. Haus des Deutschen Ostens. München, 1991.

Pistohlkors, Gert von. *Deutsche Geschichte im Osten—Baltische Länder*. Siedler Verlag, Berlin, 1994.

Raun, Toivo U. *Estonia and the Estonians*. Hoover Institute Press. Stanford University, 1991.

Samuel, Wolfgang W.E. *German Boy–A Refugee Story*. Willie Morris Books, 2000.

Staden, Berndt von. *Erinnerungen Aus Der Vorzeit–Eine Jugend im Baltikum 1919-1939*. Siedler Verlag. Berlin, 1999.

Stern, Fritz. *Five Germanys I Have Known*. Farrar, Straus & Giroux. New York, 2006.

Ungern-Sternberg, Nils Freiherr von. *Deutschbalten unter diesem Zeichen*. private printing. 1989/90.

Wittram, Reinhard. *Baltische Geschichte–Die Ostseelande Livland, Estland, Kurland 1180-1918*. Verlag R. Oldenbourg. München, 1954.